ARQUITECTONICA

ARQUITECTONICA

Foreword by Philip Johnson

Introduction and text by Beth Dunlop

Designed and edited by Massimo Vignelli

The American Institute of Architects Press
Washington, D.C.

© 1991 The American Institute of Architects
All rights reserved
Printed in Canada by D.W. Friesen
Printers through Four Colour Imports, Ltd.

3rd Printing — 1993

The American Institute of Architects Press
1735 New York Avenue, N.W.
Washington, D.C. 20006

Library of Congress Cataloging-in-Publication Data
Dunlop, Beth, 1947–
Arquitectonica
foreword by Philip Johnson
introduction and text by Beth Dunlop
design by Massimo Vignelli.
p.   cm.
ISBN 1–55835–047–0. ISBN
1–55835–043–8 (pbk.).
1. Arquitectonica (Firm : Coral Gables, Fla.)
2. Architecture, Modern—20th century—United
States.   I. Title.
NA737.A77D8   1991
720'.92'2—dc20

Type in Univers
by Graphic Composition, Inc., Athens, Georgia

Cover and jacket illustrations:
Front: The Atlantis, Miami, Florida;
photo by Norman McGrath
Back: Banco de Credito, Lima, Peru;
photo by Timothy Hursley

Contents

Foreword

The architecture firm of Arquitectonica—Bernardo Fort-Brescia and Laurinda Spear—is the gutsiest team in the business. Ever since the pink, pink house of 1978 they have fought in the front lines of avant-garde design.

One of their first buildings was almost too successful: the Atlantis in Miami, "the building with the hole in it," became the symbol of the TV series Miami Vice *and the firm's own trademark. Unfortunately it then became the landmark of Miami itself, which made it a hard act to follow. But Arquitectonica followed it with an enormous production in a very short time. Of the firm's work there is room to mention just a few examples.*

One of the most extraordinary is the huge Sawgrass Mills shopping mall in Florida. Here the architects succeeded at the almost impossible task of reducing the scale into units small enough to be comprehensible and different enough from each other to be interesting. Each sub-mall is unique in shape, with its own roof treatment and style of shop front, a variety of eclecticism that unexpectedly works well.

In contrast is the modesty of the Bank of America on Wilshire Boulevard in Beverly Hills, straightforward, urban, elegant, refined. The curved, polished granite blank wall of half the facade, "decorated" with one massive balcony, breaks the faceted mirror surface to reveal the skeletal construction of the other half.

Most important to this writer, however, are Arquitectonica's unbuilt works. Often an architect's most genial concepts are best revealed on the sketchpad. The first of these, the Maba House, planned for a very narrow Houston lot, is a straightened sequence of cubes butted together, identical in size but each unique, a brilliant plan for an only too typical downtown site.

A very different feat is the concept for Horizon Hill Center in San Antonio. The huge scale of the whole might shock the neighbors, but it excites great wonderment—one of the desiderata, surely, of good architecture. The triumphal arch has been with us for a long time. It is still a powerful example of monument as overscale.

Another strong statement is Arquitectonica's entry in the competition for the South Ferry site in New York. Their design is again a scaleless monument, a 70-story tower decorated with motifs from Constructivism and De Stijl that seem apt, clear, compelling.

The latest of these unbuilt designs is the competition drawing for the U.S. pavilion for the Seville 1992 World's Fair. Here the team could let themselves go. Freely placed ellipses cut through both plan and section, the main control "axis" runs at a slight diagonal, the wall-hung walks are very gradual ramps, the roofs are wedges. The "procession" is by very large escalators that pass one another at strange angles. The columns under the porte-cochère tip slightly. The symbolic tower is an upside-down cone. Yet the whole is a simple, even serene rectangular mass.

Arquitectonica is a young firm. Its architecture, like that of other young firms such as Steven Holl in New York and Morphosis and Eric Owen Moss in California, represents a new generation worldwide. Modern architecture is in good hands.

Philip Johnson

New York, July 1991

Introduction

by Beth Dunlop

The work of Arquitectonica is more than anything else an exploration and expression of the new. Although it has roots in early modernism, Russian constructivism, Cubism, and the more flamboyant designs of the 1950s, it is not really derivative. The relationship to the past and to place is oblique, more a metaphor or nuance than a direct statement.

Instead, the firm's work evinces movement and progress; it is a look to the future. Arquitectonica's architecture is the kind that often, at first, startles and shocks. It is buoyed by the kind of optimism that epitomized the modern movement—the belief that anything ought to be possible. It stretches both definition and reality. Many architects want their buildings to be taken literally, at face value, but with Arquitectonica what you see is not always what you get. Perception, proportion, and even the physics of gravity—generally left unquestioned since Sir Isaac Newton—are all fodder for the firm's imagination. It is an approach that entails some risk, but at the same time there is room for a bit of romance.

Part of the romance is inextricably bound up with the firm's genesis in Miami. Arquitectonica and Miami came of age almost simultaneously. In 1977 Miami was an awkward, backward city on the threshold of change; it was no longer the glamorous resort of the 1950s, and it had not yet become the center of international trade and intrigue that it is now. With its influx of Cuban and Caribbean immigrants, it was on the brink of a new identity, about to emerge as a young, vibrant, cosmopolitan city that needed to position itself culturally as well as economically. Arquitectonica International was founded at the right time.

The firm's first buildings—among them the Spear House, the Babylon, the Palace, the Atlantis, and the Imperial—were complex and colorful, abstract and audacious. They seemed to synthesize the idea of the new Miami, a city at once palpable and elusive. Arquitectonica's combination of artistic rigor and sultry romanticism was just right for the moment.

Thus, the Atlantis, with a hole punched in the middle to make way for a red jacuzzi, a yellow spiral staircase, and a tilted palm tree, became an instant symbol. The Spear House, with its glass block insets and planes of pink, makes a statement about modern life in the tropics. The captivating drawings for the Babylon were evocative and almost other-worldly. Those early buildings spoke to the mystery and the energy of Miami, capturing attention from the start.

And more than any other architectural imagery, except perhaps the Art Deco District, the architecture of Arquitectonica has come to represent Miami—in photographs and movies and on television. The firm's work rapidly became the city's hallmark. It was just six years old when Miami's Center for the Fine Arts mounted an exhibition of its work that went on to the Walker Art Center in Minneapolis and then to Houston, San Francisco, Philadelphia, and Europe.

Few firms gain so much notice for early work, but Arquitectonica's compelling, colorful new buildings were irresistible. Soon came commissions in Texas, Virginia, New York, California, Peru, France, Portugal, Luxembourg, and Holland. The firm's work now stands throughout the country and in Europe. Ultimately, Arquitectonica is much more than a Miami architectural firm; its fresh modernist vision is not confined to a single place.

But Arquitectonica's roots are undeniably in Miami and all that it represents. The firm's principal partners, Laurinda Spear and Bernardo Fort-Brescia, live there. Spear is a second-generation Miamian, educated at Brown and Columbia universities. Fort-Brescia, born in Peru, is of French and Italian descent (apt for Miami's mix of cultures) and a graduate of Princeton and Harvard.

The firm is comparatively young. Founded by five architects as a collaborative venture, it eventually dwindled to the two principals. The firm has grown and changed over the years, moving from a tiny and rather rickety walk-up studio to a full floor of an office building and from the comparatively limited challenge of simple slab condominium plans to highly involved and intricate designs.

The essential traits of both the practice and the product are still conspicuous, however—restless energy, subtlety, originality, daring. The firm's work has been marked by its insistent inquiry into several very difficult issues of architecture, among them questions of composition and contradiction.

In a generation of postmodernists, architects seeking solutions in history or classicism, Spear and Fort-Brescia have remained determined modernists. They are part of a small cadre of American architects who shunned the prevalent movements of the 1980s. "One of the aspects of our work is our persistence in exploring modernism in the times of despair for the modernists," explains Fort-Brescia. He links his firm's work with that of other American modernists—Frank Gehry in California, Antoine Predock in New Mexico, and Steven Holl in New York. "Our firm did not renege on principles of modernism but pushed forward with it."

In many ways Arquitectonica's work has as much in common with modernism in other arts—dance, literature, and painting—as it does with architectural modernism. The structures often have a powerful language, even some sexual imagery, which is generally shunned in architecture but embraced by other abstract arts such as dance. The work sometimes unfolds in a literary fashion, with wry allusions or as a series of vignettes, chapters in a book, or verses in a poem.

In the unbuilt Maba House, for example, each room is considered a "passage" and has a distinctive character. At Sawgrass Mills, a huge shopping mall, the story is told more directly. Each entrance is different; within the mall the various courts and streets take on independent personalities.

Arquitectonica makes use of simple, almost childlike forms in an incredibly complex, sophisticated way. Whimsical elements and motifs often belie a true seriousness of purpose that emerges on close scrutiny. But the scrutiny is necessary. At first glance the architecture of the Walner House in suburban Chicago, appears straightforward—deceptively so. Studied, it becomes ever more intricate, ever more inexplicable—intentionally so. Arquitectonica wanted to design a house that "would become more and more unfathomable with each passing minute."

Some of the ideas expressed by Arquitectonica's buildings are utterly poetic; others have a rough, almost agitated quality. In some both tranquility and frenzy are juxtaposed. The first is, oddly, easiest to come by; architecture is full of lessons about beauty achieved through harmony and proportion, commodity and delight. The latter is more difficult. "There is a precarious element in all our buildings," Spear observes. "It has nothing to do with deconstructionism. It's about buildings exploding."

In Arquitectonica's work buildings do more than simply sit. The language is strenuous: forms slice through one another, collide with one another. The interaction of forms is of almost anthropomorphic interest; buildings penetrate one another, one form dominates another. Large and small volumes interconnect.

At the Center for Innovative Technology in Herndon, Virginia, a horizontal structure in the form of a parallelogram is placed so that it appears to be sliding off the parking platform. This precipitous placement of forms is evident also in the Banco de Credito in Lima, Peru, certainly one of the firm's monumental achievements.

One of Arquitectonica's goals is to make the inconceivable happen—or at least seem to happen. In Rio the central square appears to be floating in a reflecting pool. In the Atlantis the middle chunk of the building was simply removed, giving the lie to the idea of building as solid mass.

"In a way, our work is about making it look like it's impossible," says Spear, "so that somebody driving by would think, 'Gosh, how'd they do that?'" Arquitectonica has explored the design of buildings that cantilever out beyond the realm of belief, "antigravity" buildings, buildings that might careen, cant, slide, slip, or tilt perilously.

The continued theme of contradiction has its roots in both art and technology. Arquitectonica's work is indeed paradoxical and provocative. Buildings do cantilever precariously and tilt unexpectedly. Structures with unlike proportions, materials, and forms are intentionally juxtaposed. In the Bank of America in Los Angeles, a thin black wall curves like paper, as if that were the only way to keep the building standing up; in the Atlantis the spiral staircase that teeters past the edge of the sky court appears to support the upper half of the building.

For Arquitectonica modernism has meant finding a new place in history rather than finding a place from history. Spear and Fort-Brescia have a general dislike of nostalgia, unless it can be used to underscore a building's anomalous qualities.

When history is in fact invoked in Arquitectonica's work, it is done in an archeological sense: A stained-glass window in the North Dade Justice Center is drawn from patchwork patterns of Florida's Miccosukkee Indians. Stone walls at the Banco de Credito are laid in the random fashion of the Incas, and the elliptical shape of the central space is derived from the pre-Columbian towers at Machu Picchu. Fort-Brescia and Spear believe in this kind of primal inquiry into a city's roots. It is a search for an idiom that springs from indigenous, not imported, culture, from a tacit memory.

Fort-Brescia and Spear have an unrelenting fascination with modern building systems, with the idea of buildings that use and celebrate technology. Their work tends to reveal certain truths rather than deny or conceal them. The Center for Innovative Technology is set in the lushly wooded hills of Virginia, but the architects decided to make a highly engineered building, even though another impulse would have been to go with the flow of the landscape. At Miracle Center in Miami trapezoidal painted panels hung from the facade are painted almost as a parody of faux marble, not a trompe l'oeil imitation of the real thing but definitely a man-made object.

Another of the firm's interests has been exploring the potential of the curtain wall as both a structural system and an artistic tool. Arquitectonica's work tries to stretch architecture as far as it will go, and one aspect of this approach is proving that the building surface can be as versatile and as full of artistic possibilities as a painter's canvas. At the Center for Innovative Technology the curtain wall has become a study in multiple colors of glass—gold, green, and black—applied in a pattern and treated almost like marble cladding. The competition entry for the Arbed headquarters, with its steel trusses, pushes the limits of structural daring and artistic expression.

In some cases the facade becomes almost an urban billboard. The three early condominiums on Brickell Avenue in Miami—the Palace, the Atlantis, and the Imperial—are buildings designed to be perceived at distances and from automobiles traveling at high speeds.

Arquitectonica's work has sometimes been regarded as anti-urban, but it actually is not. The work deals with urban realities—the automobile, the expressway, the fast pace of life—and tries to use them to advantage. The design of the North Dade Justice Center, which sits between a police station and a heliport right on U.S. 1, projects a certain civic monumentality and yet capitalizes on the rather kinetic quality of its location. The firm's small urban shopping complexes—such as Washingtonian Center in Washington, D.C., Rio in Atlanta, and Miracle Center in Miami—cater to the passing motorist as well as the pedestrian. A driver passing by Miracle Center can look right into shop windows set into the building's base. More than many other architects of this generation, Arquitectonica has understood that its buildings will be perceived by most people in two dimensions—in magazines or books and on television or film. And more so than many other buildings of this generation, Arquitectonica's work stands up to the flat, static scrutiny of the camera's lens.

But at Miracle Center the firm explored the idea of sound in architecture, moving almost in a leap to something quite beyond three architectural dimensions. The center is designed to be especially noisy to heighten the sense of activity inside it; users of the elevators experience a special sound art installation. The building represents a new level of inquiry into the sensual aspects of architecture.

Arquitectonica's buildings always start as drawings; Spear is a remarkable artist, but the Arquitectonica studio has always attracted modernists who could draw. The buildings begin life as two-dimensional studies and then are turned into visually powerful axonometrics before emerging as three-dimensional objects, whether models or actual structures.

This procedure does not imply consistency; on the contrary, the exploration into these questions veers off in many different directions, sometimes within the confines of a single project. "Our argument is, Why should a building have a single vocabulary?" says Fort-Brescia.

Building materials are used paradoxically. Glass block, for example, forms the floor of a bridge in the Center for Innovative Technology. The Bank of America uses marble where glass might be expected and vice versa. Crude, industrial materials and surfaces—mottled spray paint, dotted nonskid rubber floors, perforated steel—emerge elegant.

For Arquitectonica the building is in many ways a collage in the strongest sense of the word—Fort-Brescia cites the work of Braque, Picasso, and Leger—where forms and patterns mix with colors and shadings that become the painting. Spear, because she is an artist as well as an architect, is interested in the painterly approach to architecture, in exploring the possibilities of pictographic representation and the juxtaposition of flat surfaces and sculptural volumes.

At this level the sculptural and the pictorial intertwine in Arquitectonica's work. Form and facade interact. Simple shapes are skewed. A space that might be circular is instead almost an ellipse; a structure that would have been a square comes out trapezoidal. The middle of a building sits off-center on its base as if it had been rotated.

One fascination has always been with scale—making the big seem small and the small seem big. Several unbuilt projects, particularly the Helmsley Center and Horizon Hill, were designed at an immense scale to provoke a sense of awe. Even in the Palace the smaller, intersecting building is designed to reinforce the size of the slab tower. The double-story grid on the tower emphasizes its scale even more. In other cases, however, the idea is to manipulate the scale, to make things seem other than they are. At the sprawling Sawgrass Mills shoppers enter the mall through fifty- foot-high structures, while inside the storefronts are kept at a smaller-than-average scale to contrast with the vastness of the space.

Arquitectonica was in many ways a forerunner in the extensive use and intellectual application of architectural color. In 1982 painting a building red or blue seemed quite bold, but the rapid shifts in architecture during the mid- and late 1980s have made color an expected design element, not an audacious one.

Arquitectonica's first built work, the Spear House, with its five shades of pale and bright pinks applied to layered planes, made color integral to the design. The Atlantis has a bright blue concrete grid on its south wall, and one wall of the Imperial is painted brick-red.

Arquitectonica always uses color in a compositional way—to communicate ideas about facade or geometry and to distinguish among various building materials and forms. The Palace's bright red wing and its flat white supergrid have practical applications, to be sure, but they are also conceptual. The Imperial's floating wall was painted red for theoretical as well as practical reasons. In a way the stucco-on-concrete buildings so typical of Florida and California provide a perfect palette; with them, especially, color can be integral to the idea, not added later.

But, of course, there's a twist. Now that color is in widespread use, Arquitectonica's most recent buildings sometimes completely lack bright hues or, as is the case in the architects' own residence in Miami, have mere splashes of color against a perfectly neutral base.

From the beginning Arquitectonica's work has provoked two simultaneous responses—acclaim and resistance. The work is different and difficult enough to be challenging and open to debate. For Arquitectonica that public debate is, in a way, part of the art. A similarity to the artist Christo comes to mind. For Christo, however, the process of planning the work of art is publicly controversial. For Arquitectonica the process is private, but the product—the building—is public and often hotly debated.

The Spear House was photographed, filmed, and published in numerous American and European magazines, both scholarly and popular. At the same time it provoked its share of local controversy; it is an oddity in its suburban Miami neighborhood of traditional ranch and colonial houses. The series of town houses in Houston splashed color through a subdued residential neighborhood and offered a new look at architectural geometry.

Throughout history art and argument have gone hand in hand, of course. In Arquitectonica's work iconoclasm is an ideal, not an accident.

Even the firm's first buildings for Miami were iconoclastic—insistently colorful and boldly detailed so as to be seen from the dominant vantage points of the city. "We built them," notes Fort-Brescia, "not to be controversial, but because we believed that this was a modern city with its roots in modern times, not the 14th century."

A number of levels of daring are in operation here. One is a willingness to undertake virtually any kind of design and work with it. Indeed, during its first years of practice, Arquitectonica has willingly taken on the kinds of commonplace projects that most architects interested in esteem would shun—strip shopping centers, speculative office buildings, enclosed malls—and elevated their design beyond the commercial standard. No building type is rejected out of hand. Arquitectonica will tackle virtually anything in the continuing belief that each building can be a concept unto itself, that each building can contain and impart an idea about architecture, art, and modern society.

In its first such venture—the Square at Key Biscayne, a shopping center—Arquitectonica turned the strip into a square, just as the name implies. At Rio in Atlanta the square was given additional twists, and a new layer of artistry was added in the landscape design. But probably no project more signifies Arquitectonica's willingness to work with the mundane than Sawgrass Mills, the 2 million-square-foot discount shopping mall in suburban South Florida. Arquitectonica organized the exterior acres of parking around allées of palm trees and created individual abstract gateways for the mall's many entrances. Inside, the mall was divided into streets and courts, all set into a rather crude, factory-like superstructure.

The risk in trying to apply high design to such crass projects is the risk to reputation—that is, the chance of being regarded as superficial rather than substantive. Arquitectonica's willingness to take on such populist projects might belie its seriousness of purpose. Explains Fort-Brescia: "We also have an obsession with integrity of the design, that it shouldn't ever just be an application, but integral to the concept."

Still, Arquitectonica has never been afraid to let whimsy be a part of architecture. Cartoon-like fish floating across etched glass doors at the architects' home or ocean imagery at the International Swimming Hall of Fame can be translated into serious architectural forms. Buildings that begin rationally are tempered by intuition, by spontaneous gestures that have no real logical explanation. In the North Dade Justice Center windows are sliced-off circles, not quite half-moons. And although these windows hover over the judges' benches like halos, there is no authoritative reason for their specific shape. This approach represents Arquitectonica's belief in the use of intuition in architecture: that a space or form may simply "feel right" to the architect and further explanation is not needed.

Spear and Fort-Brescia look back at Arquitectonica's comparatively short history and see adherence to a few artistic ideas and a continued exploration of the provocative architectural questions of composition and contradiction.

Certainly, in the decades to come those questions will bear further scrutiny, and in Arquitectonica's studio the work will grow ever more complex. Arquitectonica will no doubt continue to elaborate on its earliest explorations of scale and plane, sculpture and facade—and go on trying to make the impossible seem to happen.

Selected Projects 1976–90

Spear House

**Miami, Florida
1976–78**

The Spear House, which sits at the edge of Biscayne Bay in the older Miami suburb of Miami Shores, is intended as an urban house within a suburban context. Rigorously conceived as a study in different planes, the house is painted five shades of pink, ranging from deep near-red to pale pink, which heighten the illusionistic perspective of the house and define the series of planes. Pink was chosen because it seemed to be the most tropical of all colors and at the time was rarely used.

Although the house was initially conceived as an object standing on its own, the west facade, facing the city, is scaled down; its dimensions diminish to relate to other houses on the street in an almost mathematical cadence. The east facade, designed for long-distance viewing from Miami Beach and the bay, is scaled so that it looms large. The approach is through a tropical grove—almost a tunnel—which opens to a geometric landscape with palm trees spaced regularly in a carpet of pavers.

The house has a precise sequence: the facade, the courtyard, and then the rooms, each framing a different view of the bay. The house encloses a swimming pool, which, along with the living areas, is on the piano nobile, one level above the ground. The house is narrow—only 18 feet wide—to capture the bay breezes and daylight as well.

The Spear House is more rigorously mathematical than Arquitectonica's later work, yet in many ways it is seminal, establishing a number of paths of inquiry that the firm has pursued consistently, including color and cadence.

Opposite top: The main floor of the Spear House contains most of the living areas as well as a courtyard and a pool. A guest bedroom just off the vestibule is separated from the rest of the house by a courtyard. The sequence of spaces leads from a library to an enclosed atrium, the dining room, and then the kitchen, which is separated from the laundry room by a covered terrace.

Opposite bottom: On the second floor one bedroom is separated from the other rooms by the two-story atrium below. The master bedroom complex includes a study, a terrace, and an exercise room.

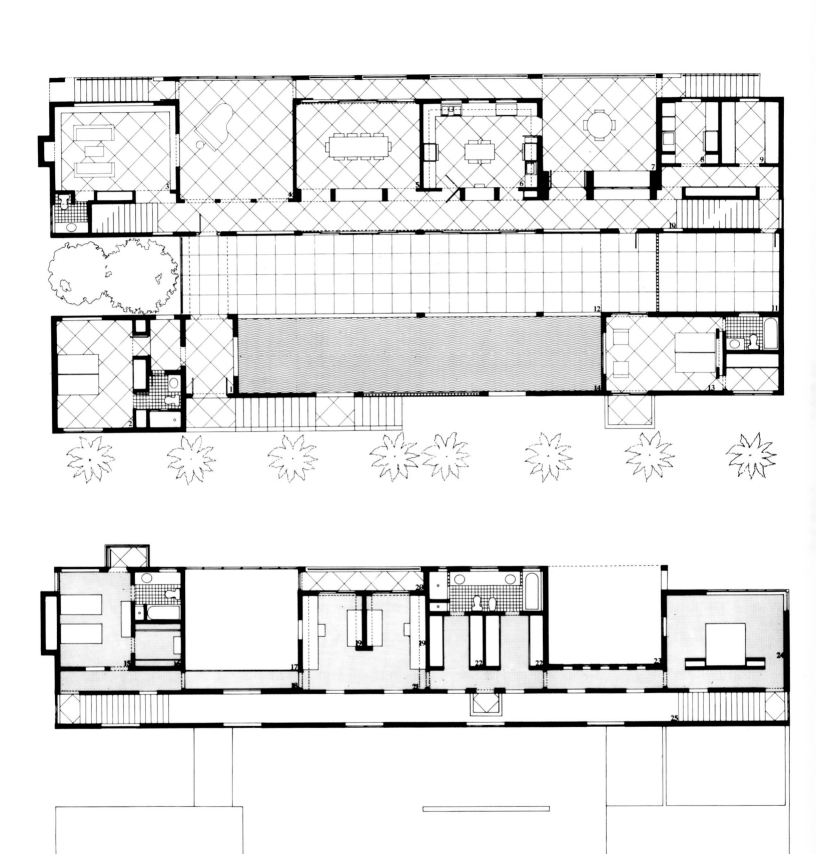

Opposite: The Spear House stands in a spare, geometric landscape.

Above: Nautical imagery, such as porthole windows, is a nod to the bayfront location of the house and to the imagery of early modernist architecture in Miami.

*Opposite and above: The long, narrow
lap pool is separated from the living
quarters by a courtyard. Both pool and
courtyard are integrated architecturally
as part of the geometric sequence, one
plane of pink following another.*

Above and opposite: The palette used in the Spear House was part of Arquitectonica's early exploration into architecture and color. In this case, it was as much an investigation of planar geometry as of color.

Babylon

Miami, Florida
1978–81

The Babylon, one of
Arquitectonica's earliest projects, is
also one of the most directly
referential to early modernist
sources. It sits on a curving corniche
roadway near Biscayne Bay in the
shadow of the Miami financial
district. A small structure nestled
into a neighborhood of high rises, it
contains only 15 apartments—one-,
two-, and three-bedroom units each
with a terrace and a view across
the street to the bay.

Designed for a wedge-shaped site,
the Babylon is a ziggurat that has
been skewed into a flattering forced
perspective. The front facade is
folded, a modification that allows
its angles to follow the curve of the
street and also serves a functional
purpose since the design had to
meet a strict city setback code.

The building has a base of local
Florida keystone, a nod to the
language of early high-rise
buildings. Its tomato-red masonry
walls are perforated by deeply
recessed vertical windows, again a
reference to early modernism.

The Babylon was depicted in·
Spear's dreamy, Chagall-like
paintings with out-of-scale lollipops
for trees and, in one, an airplane
flying across the moon. When the
building won a Progressive
Architecture award in 1978, Charles
Moore, one of the jurors, praised it
as a "reaction against many of the
other directions that are evident
today" and "for the sheer romance
of certain parts of
the plan."

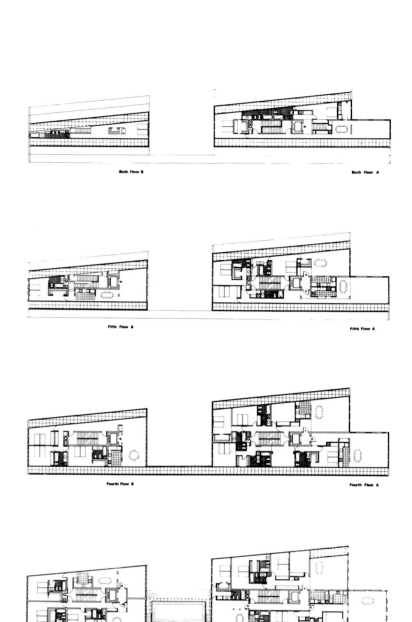

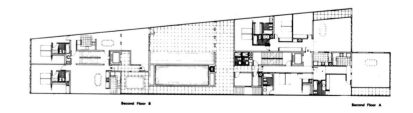

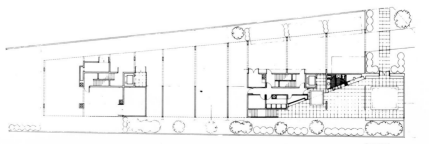

Top: The rear facade reveals the building's profile, flat rather than folded as when the building meets the street.

Bottom: The axonometric shows the triangular lot and emphasizes the Babylon's orientation to the water.

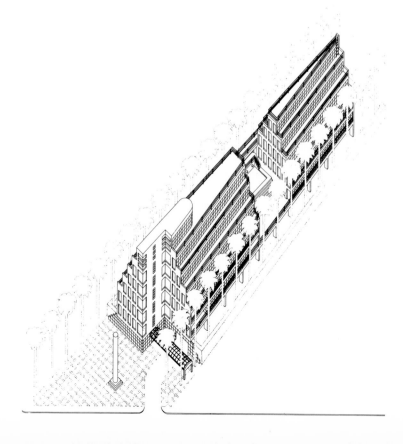

The Palace

Miami, Florida
1979–82

The Palace is sited on Biscayne Bay just south of Miami's financial district, a mile-long stretch of concrete-and-glass office buildings that is referred to as Brickell, the name of the street along which it extends. Where the street bends to follow the bay shoreline, it becomes residential. The Palace was the first of these residential buildings to be built and is the tallest condominium building in the city; it has 255 apartments on 42 floors.

Compositionally, The Palace has three elements: a main tower, a smaller terraced building intersecting the tower, and a podium lined with town houses along the waterfront. The town houses, constructed of light gray stucco with pipe-railing balconies and rooftop terraces, camouflage a two-story parking structure at the building's base.

The terrace building seems to intersect the tower, stepping up from the bay and then emerging on the other side of the building. When viewed from a distance it appears to be a giant stairway. At the front of the building, however, it becomes a monumental porte-cochère. Residents arrive along an angled driveway lined with aged royal palms, which were already on the site and were conserved.

The tower derives its scale and monumentality from the double-sized, two-story square grid. The grid emphasizes the contrast between the tower and the much shorter terrace building and distorts the reflections in the silver glass apartment windows, framing them as if they were paintings.

The main building is a thin slab tower constructed so it has three elevator cores, each serving two apartments; this configuration gives the apartments views of both the bay and the city. The three-story glass cube at the top is a single penthouse apartment.

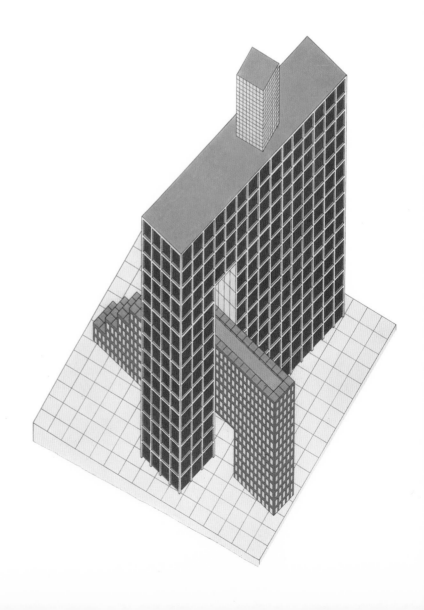

Opposite: The Palace's terrace building is intended to look quite separate, as if a small structure had intersected the larger, more pristine skyscraper.

Above: The scalar relationship of the two buildings is intentionally contrasting. The juxtaposition of scales and sense of collision of volumes are further emphasized by the collage of three distinct facade treatments—curtain wall, grid, and masonry wall with perforated openings.

Above: The Palace's double-story grid frames the curtain wall and contrasts with the punched windows.

Opposite: A complex architectural vocabulary—a convergence of three different architectural expressions—results in an unexpected conceptual clarity.

Opposite: At The Palace the intersection of the larger and smaller buildings creates a sheltered area for the swimming pool.

Above: A monumental porte-cochère dominates the entrance, exemplifying Arquitectonica's manipulation of scale and proportion.

The Square at Key Biscayne

Key Biscayne, Florida
1980–82

The Square at Key Biscayne, a neighborhood shopping center with surface parking, provides an alternative to the typical "strip" shopping center—it encloses a space rather than forming a straight line behind surface parking. The square was built as a condominium retail center with 49 shops and 6 offices. Three sides of a square, it wraps around a courtyard for parking. Its facade is layered with a colonnade that curves in front of the shops, emphasizing the frontality of the complex and giving its scale an unexpected grandeur.

Arquitectonica's first retail project, The Square shows the firm's ability to bring a fresh eye to the conventional and the commercial.

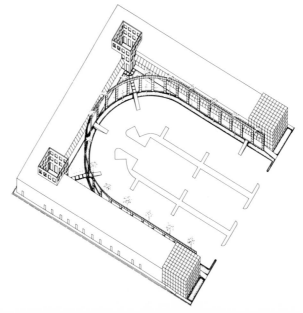

The Imperial

Miami, Florida
1981–83

The Imperial is one of three Arquitectonica projects built along the shore of Biscayne Bay on Brickell Avenue just south of downtown Miami. A 31–story condominium apartment building, it is one unit wide and 377 feet long stretching from street to waterfront. It has 156 apartments, including five duplexes at the ground level and a single penthouse on the roof. The building sits atop three levels of parking and steps down to a circular swimming pool and the waterfront.

The design is dominated by a dark-red masonry wall on the north side that appears to float alongside the building in defiance of engineering logic and gravity. The red wall rises toward the bay to give the Imperial a rooftop profile and provide a screen for the two-story penthouse, a sensuous blue stucco free-form structure. A deep blue three-story frame attached to the building creates solariums for three apartments and compositionally balances the vertical opening at the entrance.

The building was conceived as a rectangular glass "prism" to give the illusion that it is a glass structure supporting the masonry. The white horizontal banding that creates the facade on the east, west, and south sides is intended to draw the eye along the length of the building. Its practical function is to provide the parapets that form the apartment balconies and shield the apartments from the sun.

From the south side an eight-story door breaks through the building to create an unconventional entrance, drive-through lobby revealing the red wall beyond.

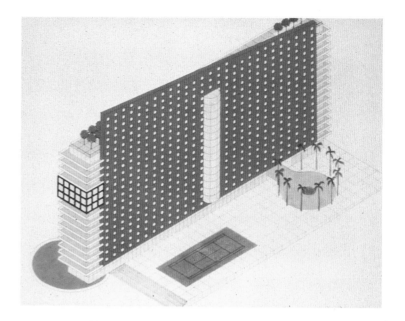

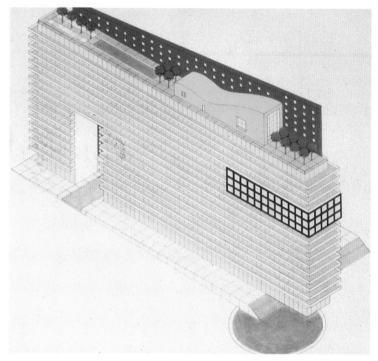

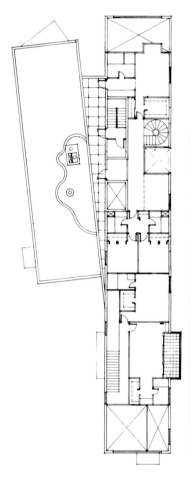

Above: Although the result is sculptural, a number of practical considerations governed the design of The Imperial. As a single-loaded corridor building, it allows through ventilation for more than half its units. The corridor, which runs along the north side of the building, is concealed by the "suspended" red wall.

Opposite: A curved vertical "stripe" in the red wall is actually balconies for the central apartments. The undulating forms on the roof hide mechanical systems.

The Atlantis

Miami, Florida
1980–82

The most photographed of all Arquitectonica's buildings, the Atlantis is a 96–unit condominium apartment building on Biscayne Bay south of downtown Miami, one of three such projects by the firm on the same street. This building, more than any other, called attention to the provocative, pictographic nature of Arquitectonica's work. It was a setting for the movie Scarface, as well as a freeze-frame image in the opening sequence of "Miami Vice." Its flat blue supergrid wall punctured by an off-center void has become an architectural symbol for both Miami and Arquitectonica.

The Atlantis is a 20–story slab building with a 37–foot-long cube cut out of the center to create a "sky court" for building residents. The sky court has three elements: a whirlpool, a red spiral staircase, and a palm tree, all set along the waving yellow wall.

The Atlantis is sited perpendicular to the waterfront so that it can easily be seen both from Brickell Avenue and from nearby Interstate 95; its imagery is simple and powerful. On the south side of the building the glass wall is covered by a three-story blue masonry grid, a brise-soleil that hides the cantilevered balconies. The gray reflective glass on the north face is punctuated by four yellow triangular balconies. The end of the building facing the bay is shaped as a nautical curve. On the other end, facing the city, a rooftop red masonry triangle conceals the mechanical equipment and provides an urban form.

The long, slender building—it is 300 feet long but only 37 feet wide—has just six apartments per floor and two elevator cores. At the bay end the building curves to create a living room with a 180–degree panoramic view. The apartments at the base are two-story duplexes with double-height living rooms and private courtyards.

When the Atlantis won a Progressive Architecture award in 1980, Frank Gehry praised it for its sculptural quality and surrealistic imagery. Helmut Jahn termed it a "rationalist, abstract building" that proposes an alternative to the lack of character in more typical new apartment buildings.

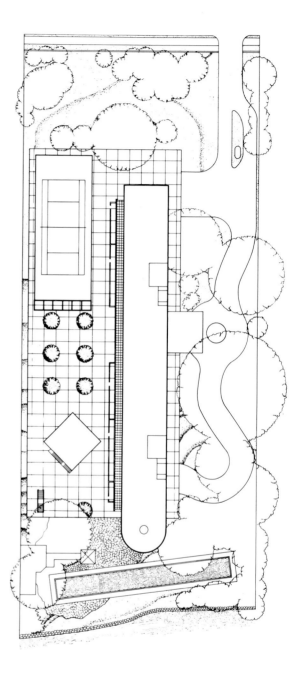

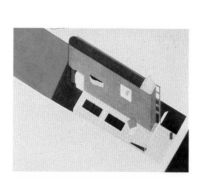

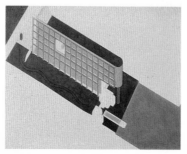

Opposite: The Atlantis was built on the site of a house that belonged to Mary Tiffany Bingham, the sister of Louis Tiffany and the wife of Hiram Bingham, the discoverer of Machu Picchu. Portions of that house have been restored as a clubhouse for condominium residents.

Above: The porte-cochère aligns with the sky court, emphasizing the building's entrance.

Above and opposite: The sky court stairway is cantilevered beyond the facade. The yellow wall hides mechanical and plumbing risers. Although the sky court is accessible to all residents, the circular staircase connects it directly to several adjacent apartments.

Opposite: A void in the middle of the building, the Atlantis sky court sits within the 12th through 17th floors. Although it measures only 37 by 37 feet, it appears larger, primarily because of its unexpected location. Because it links the masonry wall with the solid glass wall that faces north, it works to define and unify the building.

Overseas Tower

Miami, Florida
1980–82

This seven-story office building, headquarters for an international trading and finance company, is located on a waterbound "peninsula" in flat lands west of Miami International Airport. It is another of Arquitectonica's early examinations of "mixed media": a thin masonry slab is juxtaposed against a glass cylinder. Sparse landscaping emphasizes the larger-than-expected scale, even though it is a comparatively small structure. A squared-off arch is actually a drive-through banking window. A two-story sky terrace has been incorporated on the sixth floor.

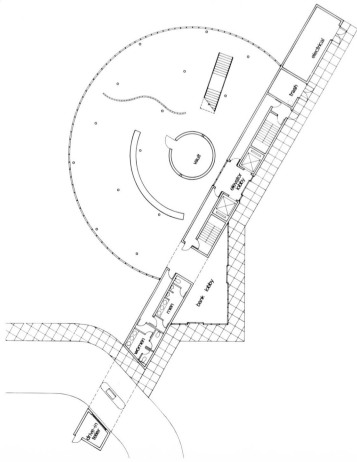

Decorative Arts Plaza

Miami, Florida
1980–82

This low-slung, 67,000–square-foot building, renovated by Arquitectonica, was designed for Miami's Design District, an urban shopping district in the middle of the city. It includes showrooms and a small art gallery, all set back under a masonry grid. Freestanding pylons define a walkway and abstract geometric forms become small pavilions within the plaza.

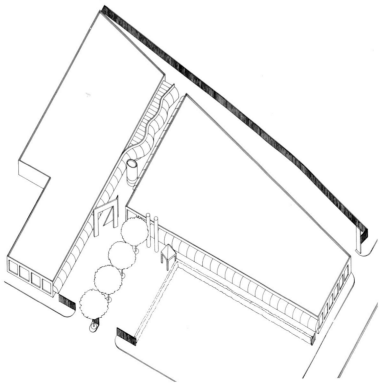

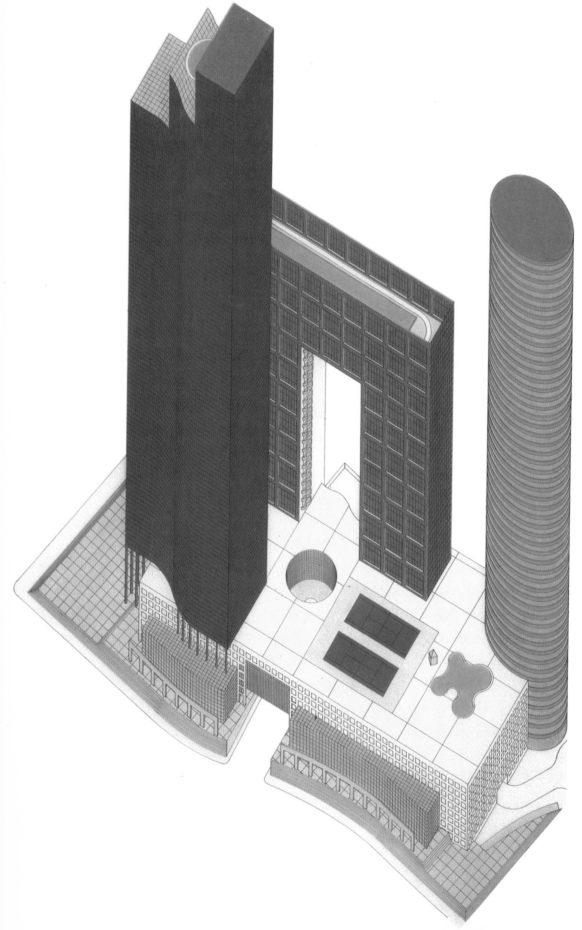

The Helmsley Center

(Design proposal)
1981

This unbuilt project of about 1.5 million square feet was to be the largest mixed-use waterfront development in Miami. The design for the three-structure complex features towers of 65, 55, and 39 stories and includes apartments, offices, shops, and a hotel. The center would have been the final link with Arquitectonica's other Biscayne Bay high rises.

The three towers are designed to rest on a five-story platform containing town houses and multiple parking levels, as well as retail shops along the street. The podium is eroded to preserve a view of the bay.

An arch created by connecting two 36–story towers forms a monumental gateway to Biscayne Bay. The building has a trussed concrete horizontal span with a pool and a running track on top.

The taller tower, a subtly curving building with a glass core, is positioned at a corner of the complex. It is designed for offices on the lower levels and a hotel above. The second tower is an elliptical structure containing 120 apartments.

Maba House

(Design proposal)
1982

This unbuilt house for a site in Houston was conceived as a series of cubes. Each cube has a different function: entrance, living room, dining room, kitchen, bedroom, and garage on the ground floor and guest room, master bedroom, and deck on the second floor.

Arquitectonica thought of each of these cubes as a passage, radically changing in character from one to another, even in the furnishings. The garden, also conceived as a series of "rooms," changes its character with each cube as well. A swimming pool parallel to the house connects the gardens.

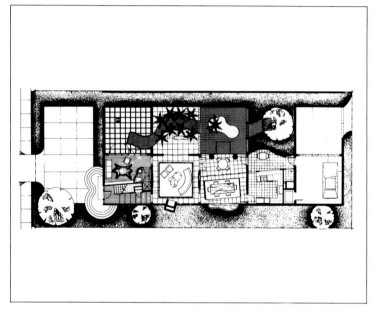

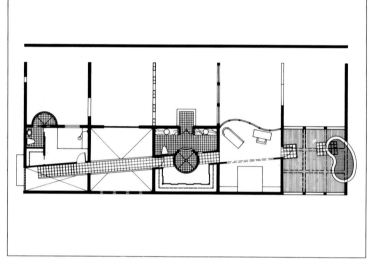

The plan was designed for an extremely narrow lot that ran from the street to an alley. The front facade was left intentionally blank so that passersby would have no idea of what was inside.

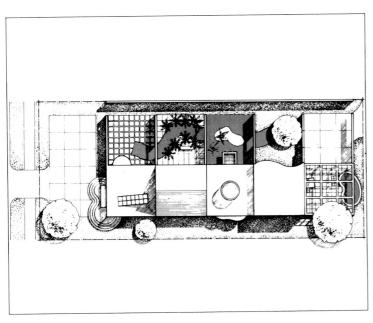

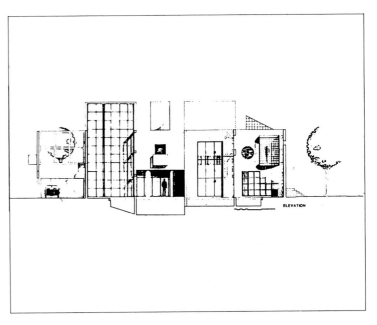

ELEVATION

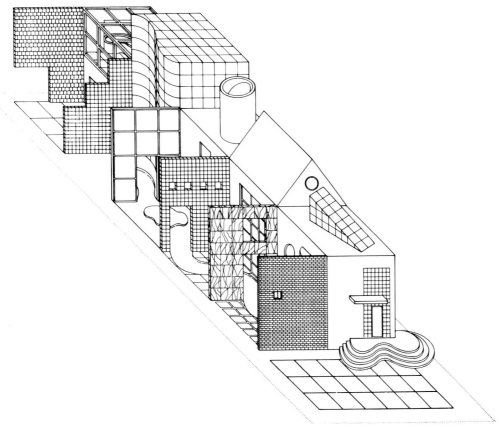

Taggart
Townhouses

Houston, Texas
1982–83

These four town houses sit on a
corner lot across from a large park.
The site allows for identical units at
each end, a square corner town
house, and an L-shaped house that
faces two streets. In addition to
shape, color and size further
differentiate the units. The end
town house elevations are grids in
cream-colored masonry, while a
corner unit is a salmon-colored cube
with varied fenestration. The L-
shaped town house is a series of
turquoise free-form terraces.

Balconies and terrace walls in each
unit extend the living areas to the
outdoors; the curvilinear walls
ensure privacy. The ground floor for
each town house contains the
bedrooms and a private garden.

The living areas are on the second
floor to provide a view of the park.
The living rooms are two stories
high with a rotated volume—a
house within a house that contains
a kitchen at the lower level and a
mezzanine loft.

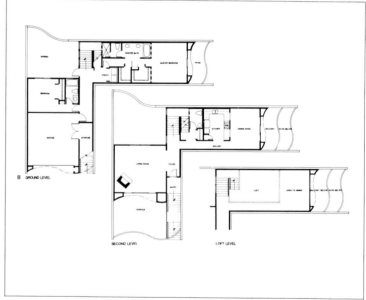

The Taggart Townhouses fit together like a three-dimensional puzzle, with four units in three different shapes. The corner unit is the most prominent; the others seem to slide into place.

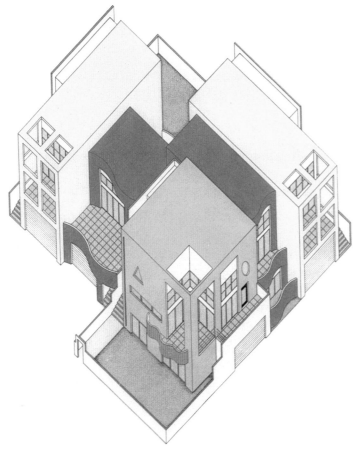

Haddon Townhouses

Houston, Texas
1982–83

Below and opposite: The yellow wall on the exterior of the Haddon Townhouses reappears inside and defines the circulation zone for each house.

These ten town houses, three stories tall, line two sides of a busy street. Eight units have angled roof lines, a play on the shed roof often used for town houses; the end units have flat roofs that step back on the sides. A yellow wall crosses through each unit to create an internal facade facing the skylit stairway space; this wall pierces the building to become a vertical element in the composition of the front facade. On the upper level a cantilevered blue window box appears as a second intersecting volume. The buildings are white with accents of primary colors. The two-story living rooms have balcony dining rooms.

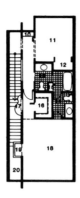

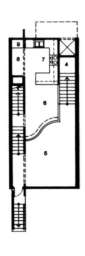

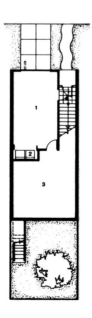

Horizon Hill Center

(Design proposal)
1982

This monumental colonnade of a building, an unbuilt project for a site in San Antonio, Texas, was to have a hotel and health club in one leg and offices in the other three as well as on the top. A retail shopping mall was planned for the base. The giant arches were designed to rise over a six-story parking podium with restaurants and recreation facilities; tennis courts cantilever over a "street of shops" that slices through the platform. A private club looks out on its own esplanade at one end of the building.

The glass-clad "monumental arcade" was conceived to frame views of downtown San Antonio. Although the project never went beyond the conceptual phase, it embodies several characteristics of Arquitectonica's work, including experimentation with scale and the use of voids to create form.

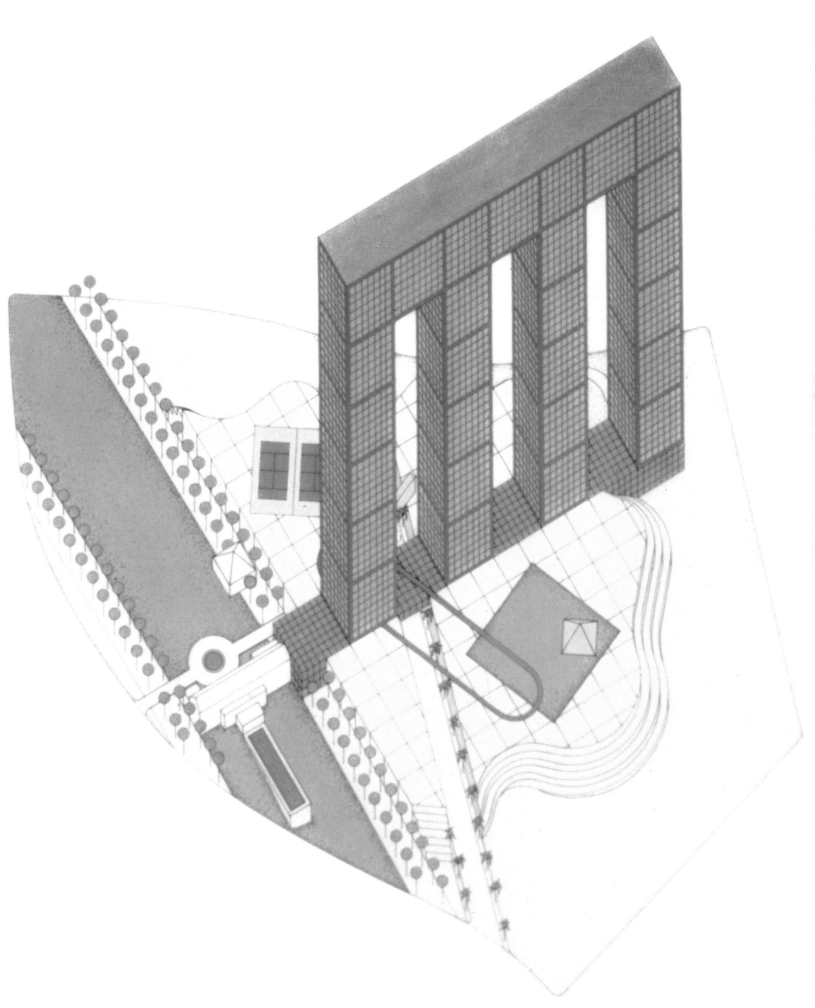

Banco de Credito del Peru

Lima, Peru
1983–88

Nestled at the foot of the Andes in the suburban section of La Molina, this headquarters building for the largest private bank in Peru surrounds an Inca burial ground and rock formations. The Banco de Credito is abstract and modern yet rooted in Peruvian history and responsive to the terrain. A four-story marble building raised on white marble pilotis, it powerfully juxtaposes rich materials against the spectacular, rugged landscape.

The facade, accentuated by strip windows of blue glass without mullions and diagonal squares of native black marble, is at once patterned and sculptural, punctuated by windows that project in various geometric forms—triangles, squares, semicircles, and rectangles.

Underneath, behind the row of steel columns, various forms and volumes appear to slide under the building. Although sculptural in effect, each has a practical function—to house the banking hall, the cafeteria, the auditorium, and the public areas of the corporate complex. Other forms appear to slice through the building; clad in white marble and white stucco, they house the boardroom, stairwells, and offices of the department heads. An elliptical glass block volume serves as the main lobby.

The organization of the building, with its formal exterior public facade and more informal interior facades, recalls traditional Peruvian courtyards. The courtyard facade is clad in locally quarried pink slate cut in irregular slabs. Square windows of green-tinted glass are set randomly. The linear building surrounding the square courtyard is interrupted only by the hillside penetrating the center court.

The 530,000–square-foot project includes a 70,000–square-foot computer center, two restaurants, an auditorium, a rooftop health club, and a coin museum. The building also is designed to accommodate a high-technology security system and state-of-the-art electronic data transmission equipment. For security reasons, all public functions are at the ground level and can be accessed without entering the main building.

The interior, which has an open plan, provides orientation points: cylindrical elevator lobbies and distinctively shaped walls focused on the courtyard.

The architects designed the carpets, paneling, and much of the office furniture (including desks and credenzas) using local craftsmen and a color scheme derived from traditional Inca palettes.

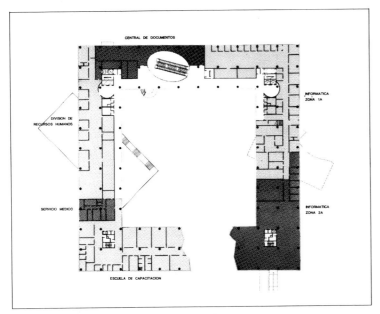

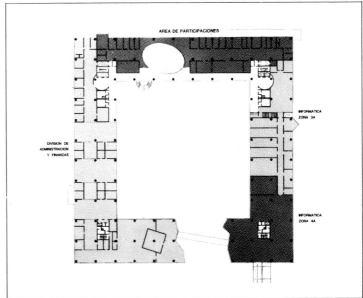

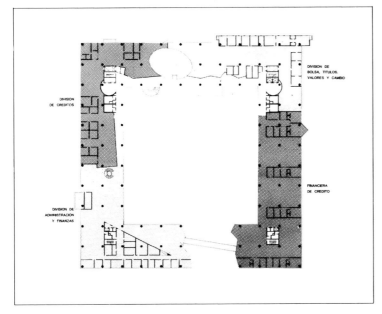

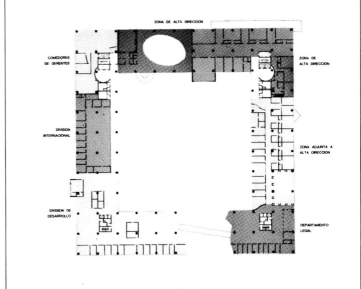

Each department has its own character. The architects created "neighborhoods" within the 120,000–square-foot levels, giving different areas individual identities. These zones are self-contained, making departments in the bank seem like small private companies.

The plan allows for circulation throughout the offices. Corridors of varying dimensions and character lead from department to department. Stairs link upper and lower floors and provide an alternative to elevators.

Above: The bank's setting—the foothills of the Andes—had a pronounced influence on the way the building was positioned. Its taut exterior of glass and marble is intended to communicate financial stability and the importance of the bank as an institution, but it is humanized by the volumes that break up the exterior and enliven the composition.

The bank dominates the smaller, simpler buildings that surround it, but it in turn is overpowered visually by the Andes, the source of the country's wealth and culture.

Opposite and above: The ground level of the Banco de Credito is as important as the principal floors; it reveals the volumes that intersect the building and provides a perspective of its most sculptural aspect. It also accommodates the activities that require public access; regular banking and meetings are held on the ground floor.

Above: Although many elements of the Banco de Credito are staid and monumental, some are more daring, almost inexplicable; for example, a stairway cantilevers out from a stone wall and a stone bridge rests on two zigzag glass walls.

Opposite: The transparent quality of the ground level allows the viewer to understand the building above and see the floor plan revealed.

Opposite: The Banco de Credito is set against the Andes, and the mountains become the building's backdrop and symbol.

Above: The courtyard of the Banco de Credito is made of native stone, a pink slate, laid in a random pattern based on the intricate and elaborate patterns of the Incas. The arrangement of the windows looking out on the courtyard also appears random.

Above: The boardroom has walls made of wood paneling in an Inca pattern and a sloping roof that makes possible a broad view of the Andes. The idea here was to give the room a prominent position and yet let it be a part of the landscape as well.

Opposite: With its deep-set windows of different sizes and shapes and its varied roofline, the Banco de Credito has a powerful silhouette. Its strong geometry and rich texture seem enhanced against the night sky.

Opposite and above: The entrance hall of the Banco de Credito, a dramatic elliptical space made of glass block and topped by a skylight, intersects the building vertically.

Above: The waiting room outside the boardroom is distinctive as the only instance in which a cylindrical volume is sliced open to reveal the entire space around it.

Opposite: The rugs in the boardroom, manufactured in Peru, were designed by Arquitectonica using colors found in the Incas' feathered capes.

Mandell Townhouses

Houston, Texas
1982–84

Although these town houses are a study in composition, each unit has a separate identity. The four units are built of pale red brick with brightly painted highlights. The front doors, window frames, and garage doors are painted bright blue, and the chimneys and overhangs are painted bright yellow. Each of the four connected units has a distinctive facade. One end unit has a white double cutout window. Next to it, a shorter unit has a distended gable along its facade. Another unit has a regular grid of square windows, and its facade rises to a parapet with square cutouts. The final unit has an arrangement of two square windows topped by a triangular one.

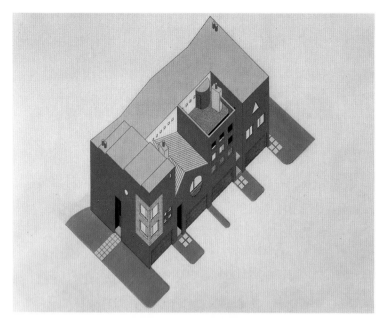

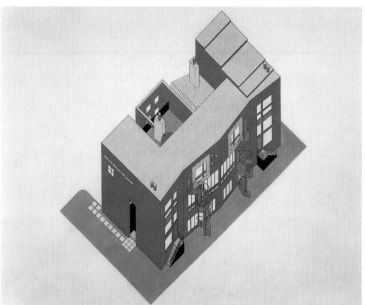

Mulder House

Lima, Peru
1983–85

A tall white stucco wall shields this family house from passersby, providing privacy. The house itself is placed on an angle within a narrow lot, so that the view out is at an angle. Two intersecting walls create a framework for the house, dividing it into four quadrants, each with its own function, form, and orientation.

The first quadrant, a sculptural form that serves as the introduction to the house, is a two-story entry foyer with a mahogany stair, a hand-cut slate floor, and glass blocks imbedded in a pink-colored stucco wall. The entryway is capped by a floor-to-ceiling skylight. The second quadrant is the living room; it forms the shape of a segment of an ellipse and has floor-to-ceiling glass without mullions as its perimeter wall. A red fireplace supports the thin roof slab.

The third quadrant, which is two stories, contains the family's sleeping quarters upstairs and a dining room and library downstairs. The library is separated from the rest of the house by an exterior breezeway, thus providing a quiet workplace; it is also connected to the master bedroom suite by a cantilevered yellow staircase. The final quadrant consists of the kitchen and servants' quarters downstairs and a guest bedroom upstairs. The two intersecting walls, the dominant architectural element, have sculptural cutouts to emphasize their thinness and linear quality, create plays of light and shadow, and frame special views of the four gardens.

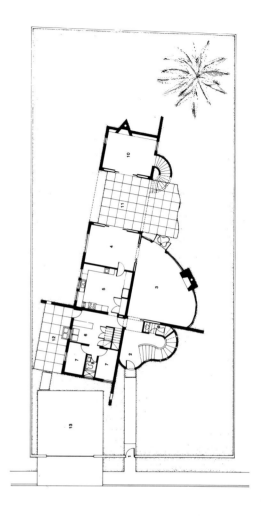

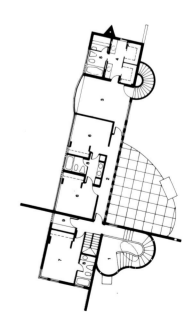

North Dade Justice Center

Miami, Florida
1984–87

This regional courthouse sits between an environmentally protected mangrove preserve and the busy highway U.S. 1. It is a two-story structure sited and shaped to respond to these dual elements in its environment while imparting a sense of civic significance.

The Justice Center is composed of three architectural volumes. A wall of green stucco and black tile encloses a protected parking area. The lobby is a rounded triangle in plan with curved walls clad in vertical panels of pink marble and green glass. The main structure, which rests on top of the other two sections, is a curved slab that widens at one end like a hockey stick.

The convex side of the building, which can be seen from the highway, is meant to be viewed at high speed. The concave side, which faces the mangroves, creates a space that embraces the trees and the lake to provide a meditative environment. A straight path connects the highway with the entrance breezeway and the lake. The path ends in a pier that intersects an environmental sculpture by Ellyn Zimmerman.

Among the special details is a drive-in payment window for parking tickets. The ground level houses the lobby and offices of the clerk, public defender, and state's attorney. An irregularly gridded black-and-white terrazzo floor emphasizes the dynamism of the spaces. An escalator and a stair leading to the second floor penetrate a jagged opening in the ceiling. The judges' chambers, courtrooms, and hearing rooms line the second-floor corridor. Yellow tile-framed clerestory windows as well as semicircular windows bring natural light into the courtrooms and jury deliberation rooms.

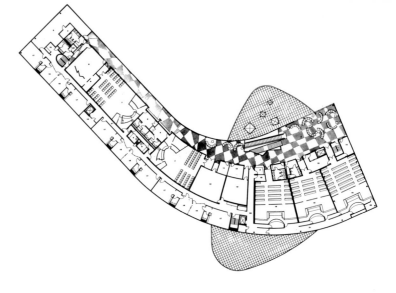

South Ferry Plaza Center

(Competition entry)
1984

This design proposal was submitted for a competition for a mixed-use development adjacent to the Staten Island ferry terminal on the southernmost tip of Manhattan. The project includes a 70–story tower with office space, hotel rooms, a conference center, restaurants, and an observation deck, as well as the construction of a new ferry terminal and the renovation of the historic Battery Maritime Building. The tower, designed to be built on piles over the river, rises on a rock base that is cut away to reveal a futuristic glass building. The lower floors of the tower accommodate hotel rooms; the upper floors are office space. The building flares out as it rises to allow for larger floor areas. An observation deck tops the building, cantilevered out over the ferry departure lanes and toward Manhattan. A gold-colored transmission tower and other sculptural forms add to the tower's futuristic image.

Creditbank Tower

Miami, Florida
1985–86

This is a 14–story speculative office building on Biscayne Boulevard north of downtown Miami, a transitional section of the city that is not heavily developed. A lobby and a branch banking center share the ground floor. The Creditbank building is a white-painted masonry structure with one wall that sweeps into a curve. Two glass-clad columns, which are actually round offices, seem to support the gridded, L-shaped facade.

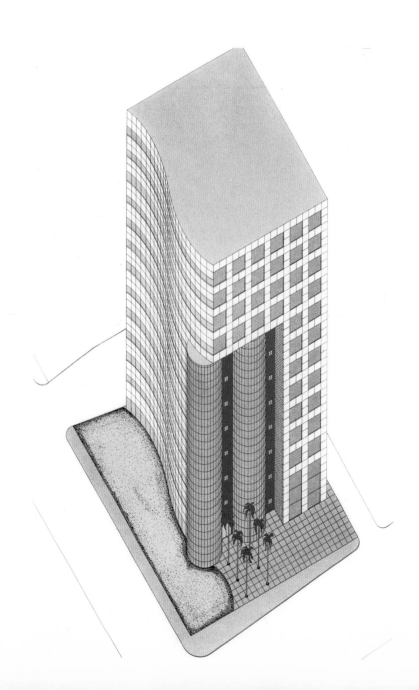

Walner House

Glencoe, Illinois
1985–87

This house, sited where a ravine meets Lake Michigan, had a threefold mandate: It must be one story, take full advantage of a spectacular site, and provide space for a private art collection. The intention was to give the house a sense of dynamic movement.

The structure's irregular Z shape is a response to the unusual site—a heavily wooded knoll rising 65 feet to a large grassy plateau. The house sits at the top, and the site allows it to front in three directions. The shape also forms a paved entry court and defines a grassy lawn that looks toward the lake. The service wing parallel to the main building provides privacy, separating both house and garden from its neighbors.

The house is a study in expressionist geometry: Although it is logical, even insightful, in response to the site, it also is planned to seem as relaxed and unintentional as possible. The architects did not seek symmetry and order: they opted for the random, odd-shaped window to frame a special view, the interrupted cadence to emphasize the natural setting.

Marble and granite-clad planes and volumes intersect the main volume unexpectedly. The intersections, although rigorously designed, are intended to seem almost accidental. The roof lifts and tilts to make rooms seem less uniform inside; it slides up over walls and cants over the master bedroom, which faces the lake. An exercise room, made of boulders, seems to break through a glass wall. A stucco prism with trapezoidal windows encloses the swimming pool.

The house is clad predominantly in pink granite in a random pattern of polished and honed finishes. In addition it has black granite bases and planes of black, white, and green marble. Floors throughout are maple. With the exception of the window mullions, which are stained white, the house is made entirely of natural materials and natural colors, but these are materials and colors at nature's outer limit.

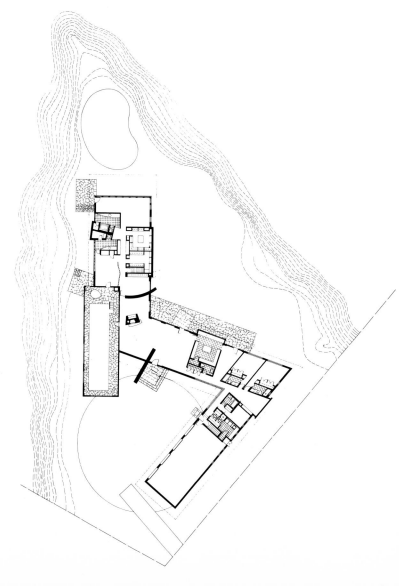

Top: The facade of the Walner House is a testimony to the richness of the materials used—the black granite at the base, the flamed and polished pink granite of the facade, the bluestone of the terrace, and the variety of marbles, including green and white marble with heavy gold veining.

Bottom: The house is indeed a modernist creation, but it has its roots in the region. Its horizontal overhangs are an allusion to the prairie house and its place in architectural history.

Opposite: The mandate for the interiors of this house was to provide ample display space for the clients' art collection yet yield to their active lifestyle. To translate this goal into aesthetics, the architects chose a natural palette and natural materials.

Above: The exterior black granite base becomes a border inside. The carpet in the master suite was custom designed by Arquitectonica in a pattern derived from the site plan of the house.

Rio

Atlanta, Georgia
1985–87

Rio is a retail center located on a busy intersection just west of Atlanta's growing downtown and midtown areas. This 100,000–square-foot complex is actually a series of structures around a central entertainment court conceived as a small urban village with detached buildings. The two-story buildings take advantage of a sloping site and allow pedestrians to move easily through the complex with access at both levels to restaurants, cafes, nightclubs, and specialty stores. One building within the complex is rotated to create the entrance.

The buildings are clad in bright blue corrugated metal siding hung vertically and have white window mullions and yellow overhangs. The rotated building has horizontal corrugated black metal siding with green mullions.

The entertainment court is a series of similarly rotated squares. The middle structure seems to float in a reflecting pool within which are set an elevator, a wet bar, a 40–foot stand of bamboo, and a "video wall." Conceived by the artist Dara Birnbaum, the wall consists of 25 television screens superimposing imagery on a video backdrop showing the site before the shopping center was constructed.

Landscape architect Martha Schwartz, with Arquitectonica, created a garden for the central court area. It is a patterned series of stripes—turf alternating with boulders—that slope into the reflecting pool. Once the stripes meet the pool they continue as fiber optics. The garden also includes a grid of golden frogs that face a vine-covered geodesic sphere.

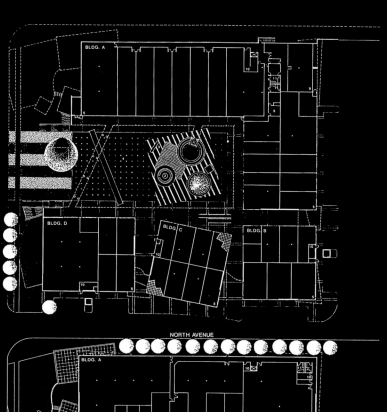

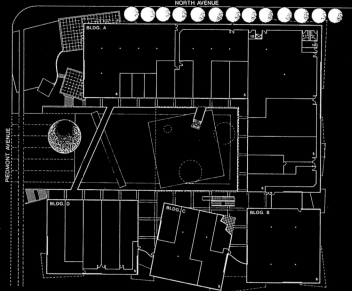

This structure is a mixed-use complex on a busy urban boulevard in Miami near Miracle Mile. It is a block-long, seven-story building that includes shops, a 10–screen movie theater, restaurants, and a health club. Miracle Center sits right on the sidewalk; passing motorists can look at merchandise displayed in retail shop windows. Three parking levels sit atop the three-level mall. The stone-blue facade, made of painted stucco on concrete, has huge, marble-like trapezoidal panels hung askew across it, floating like geometric clouds. The veining in the black-and-white "marble" is obviously artificial.

Inside, the central mall area extends the length of the block. The mall is designed as a three-story atrium with upper-level spaces, such as the health club, looking over the lower-level shopping areas. The glass elevators incorporate a visual and acoustical kinetic sculpture by Christopher Janney.

Center for Innovative Technology

Herndon, Virginia
1985–88

The Commonwealth of Virginia sponsored the development of this office and research complex in suburban Washington, D.C. The Center for Innovative Technology was created to encourage technology transfer in Virginia; the Software Productivity Consortium is a computer research group. The two institutions share a common facility in a striking natural setting on the crest of a densely wooded hill.

The complex consists of an office tower, research facility, commons, and parking garage, which serves as a base for the other three buildings. The trapezoidal, four-story garage slices through the hilltop, eliminating the need for parking lots and preserving the forest to its edge. Its gray-black metal grid cladding lets air and light in but makes the structure only a dark shadow in the forest.

The CIT Tower, located at the highest point of the site, has become a visual symbol of the complex. Its dimensions increase as it rises to give the impression of height and to imply vertical movement. Clad in a random, marble-like pattern of gold, green, and black glass, it contains CIT's offices and research areas.

The second structure, the SPC Building, houses offices and a large computer facility for software research. Its floor areas needed to be large, so the structure is horizontal. Its parallelogram-shaped form is placed to seem as if it is sliding off the parking platform. Its silver, blue, and black glass cladding is set in a random pattern, with the panels placed horizontally to emphasize the direction of the building.

The commons, which links the buildings, contains a main lobby area, exhibition gallery, auditorium, cafeteria, classrooms, and briefing room. A clear glass prism in the shape of a partial circle contains the lobby and the gallery; it is intersected by a white marble parallelogram that houses the auditorium. The materials used in the commons reflect the complex's technological preoccupation: stainless steel, glass block in the form of a bridge that seems to float, and cantilevered glass railings.

The silhouette of the complex is dramatic when seen from a distance yet from close up it provides a smaller-scale play of reflections and colors, changing as the seasons do. The plaza atop the garage, designed with landscape architect Martha Schwartz, is landscaped in a striped pattern of native Virginia stone and gravel. A circle of yellow twig dogwood punctuates the pattern of the podium, and a sunken courtyard leads to the cafeteria.

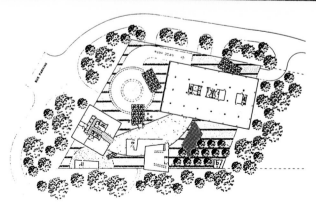

Below: Arquitectonica wanted to make it very clear that the forms of the Center for Innovative Technology are man-made. Thus, the structures are pure geometry, presented in contrast with the purposely untouched surroundings. The image is that of the machine in the forest, and high-tech materials are used to reinforce the idea of a dialogue between humans and nature. While keeping the dialogue balanced, Arquitectonica wanted the buildings to seem highly technological, even to appear to defy gravity.

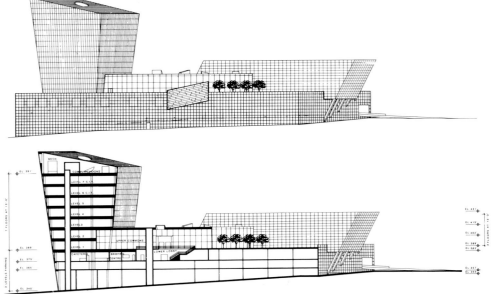

Top: The auditorium is a parallelogram completely clad in white granite and seeming to float over the black shadow of the dark "egg-crate" garage cladding.

Bottom: A transparent curving exhibition gallery links the two main volumes of the Center for Innovative Technology.

Above: In the design for the center, Arquitectonica explored the potential of the curtain wall as an artistic device by applying glass in several different colors.

Above right: Other explorations included the patterning of the deck at the entrance and the man-made landscape on the rooftop plaza over the parking plinth.

Opposite: The imagery of the lower
lobby at the center is that of technology
at work. The connecting walkways have
floors of glass block.

Above: The ceremonial entrance to the
exhibition hall is a glass volume
intended to bring the outdoors inside
and vice versa.

Kushner House

Northbrook, Illinois
1986–88

The house, with its 8,000 square feet,
presents an almost barnlike mass.
Inside, the exterior form is reflected in a
very large open space.

Located in a developing area of
suburban Northbrook, this house sits
on a three-quarter-acre site at the
edge of a pond. Designed to look
across the water to a forest
preserve beyond, it has an H-shaped
plan to create private outdoor areas
sheltered from both neighboring
houses and the northwest winds.
Each stroke of the H is a seemingly
separate house, each clad in a
different color and pattern of brick
with a distinctive geometry for its
window openings and different floor
material within—ebonized oak,
stone, and carpet.

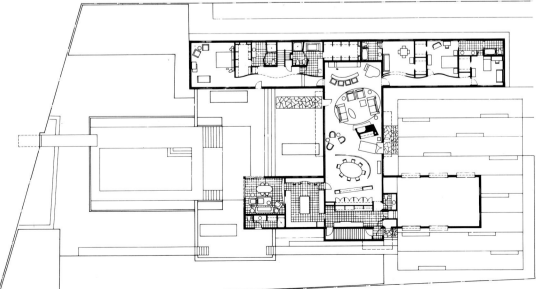

Above: The large interior spaces of the Kushner House are richly clad in a varied spectrum of materials.

Below: In plan, the house is in the shape of an H, which allows for an intimate space between the wings as well as vast vistas from the windows on the outside.

Sawgrass Mills

Sunrise, Florida
1987–90

Sawgrass Mills is a 2.4 million-square-foot discount outlet mall in Sunrise, a suburb of Fort Lauderdale, Florida. It sits on a 200–acre site and includes 11,500 parking spaces. From the start Arquitectonica grappled with the issue of the mall's enormous size and ways to prevent monotony and anonymity. The mandate was to make Sawgrass Mills at once friendly and comprehensible. Thus, parking is organized around distinctly different entrances— including a pink stucco grid pierced by gray cylinders, a cube of blue fishnet, and a yellow zigzag scaffold—each visually connected to the landscaped "fields" of cars by an allée of palm trees.

The interior organization revolves around a series of "courts," basically enclosed plazas. Each court has a different shape and a different roof form—pyramid, rotunda, or vault. This interior design is a showcase for Arquitectonica's spirited, sculptural modernism. The Video Court has two 16–screen multi-image televisions high against a bright blue wall and two dramatically placed windows—a full-circle "sun" and a half-circle "moon"— set in a coral-colored wall. The Cabana Court has a tensile white tent roof and washed-wood walls suggesting driftwood.

The shopping concourses bear distinct local architectural themes. Whimsical, three-dimensional objects in keeping with the concourse's theme are suspended from trusses to give the mall an even more celebratory, parade-like feel.

Two food courts use other themes: one is a sports court and the other, with kiosks and signs askew, depicts a hurricane sweeping through.

Structurally, the mall uses a metal building system. The architects chose to keep the framework simple and nearly industrial—it has a metal roof and wood floors—as if this were an old mill adapted to a new use.

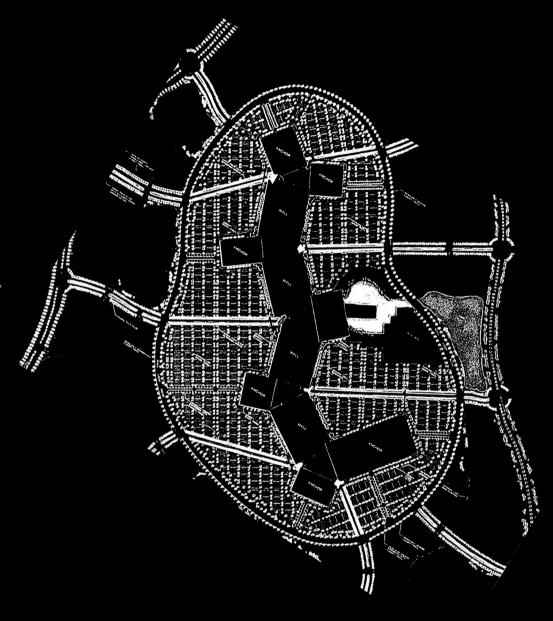

Each entrance has a unique identity to guide shoppers from their cars into the shops. The entrances have different geometries, colors, materials, and structural styles.

One entrance is a huge blue fishnet
"cube." From a distance the cube seems
almost ephemeral, but on closer view it
materializes as a sturdy structure.

Opposite: The lagoon at the Cabana Court features animated alligators and talking toucans, pelicans, and flamingoes—a little sideshow. And indeed, there is a certain debt to Disney throughout Sawgrass Mills— well-learned lessons about the way people perceive space and move through it.

Above: Inside the mall Arquitectonica created a series of "streets" linked by dramatic courts at each juncture. Each shopping street has its own theme based on an architectural style. The shops that line these streets have storefronts in keeping with the theme and at pedestrian scale. The storefronts are slightly smaller than typical mall storefronts to accommodate full facades—turrets, parapets, and eaves. Green-painted palm fronds form a backdrop behind these little streetscapes. Some facades project; others are set back.

In all there is a mile of corridors, and more than 200 shops line these hallways. Spoofy two-dimensional seahorses, beach towels, binoculars, and high-heeled shoes as well as other objects hang from high ceilings. The center's logo is a hungry saw-toothed alligator, a visual play on the center's name.

Vintage Park

Foster City, California
1987

Vintage Park is one of the first attempts at introducing high-density, high-rise housing in suburban San Francisco in response to a need for affordable rental housing in the Bay Area. The complex is adjacent to the commercial and office district of Foster City, which is midway between San Francisco and Silicon Valley near the airport and the entrance to the San Mateo Bridge. It will contain 2,500 units of housing for a range of income levels on a 34–acre site. Foster City was conceived as a Venetian city with canals and waterways, and Vintage Park is surrounded by a lake.

The complex fronts on Third Avenue, a heavily travelled commuter road; behind it is a park. The buildings, which are clustered in "neighborhoods," all sit on top of a landscaped podium that conceals a 6,000-car parking garage conceived as a giant "barge" on Vintage Lake. The garage creates an artificial new ground plane for the project; the raised ground level affords pedestrians views of the bay and the San Francisco skyline. Three sides of the garage are camouflaged by town houses; the Third Avenue elevation is a 950-foot-long waterwall. The top of the garage podium is divided into a grid to separate automobile and pedestrian traffic and is crossed by a crescent-shaped wall. The grid creates courtyards, streets, sculpture gardens, flower gardens, and playing fields.

Below and left: Five major building types are represented in Vintage Park. Four large slab buildings straddle two blocks. Four elliptical towers with blue-tiled, striped parapets cantilever over the Third Avenue waterwall. In one section a group of midrise buildings forms a courtyard with a grotto centerpiece. Town houses line the crescent walkway leading to the high-rise office building, shaped like a giant robot or transformer.

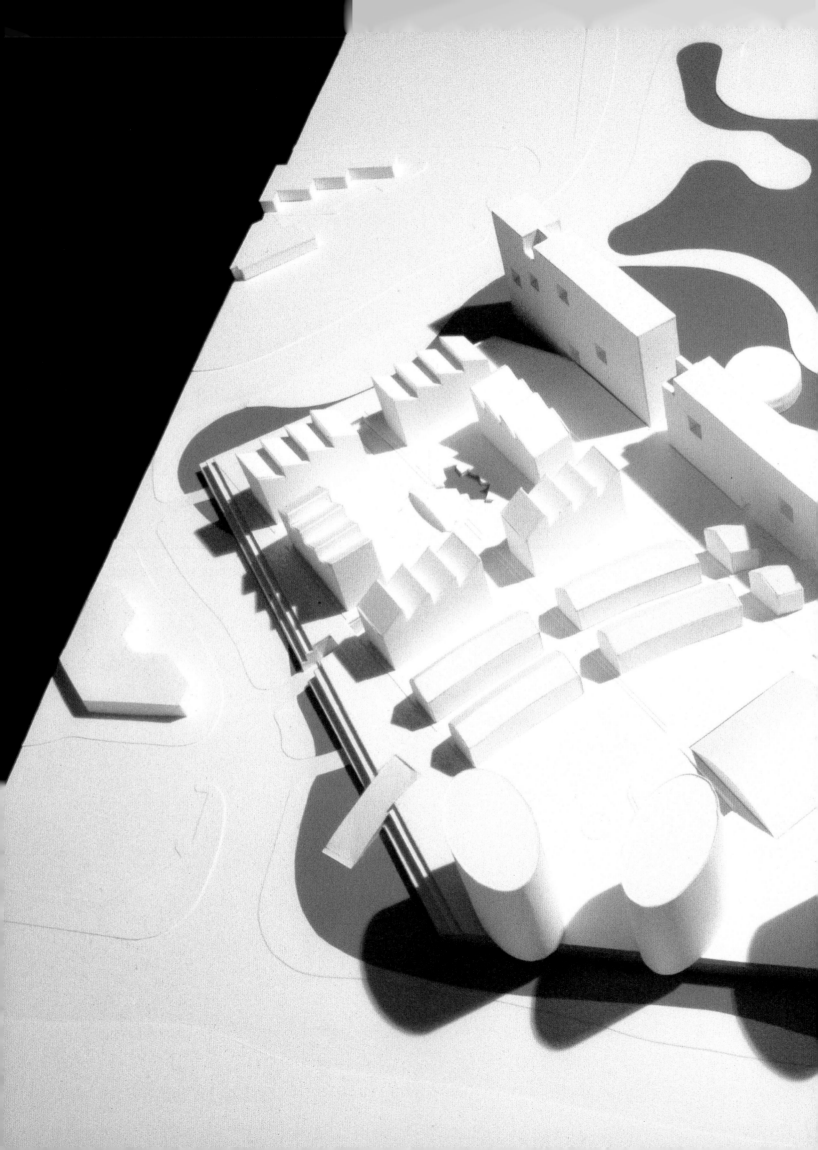

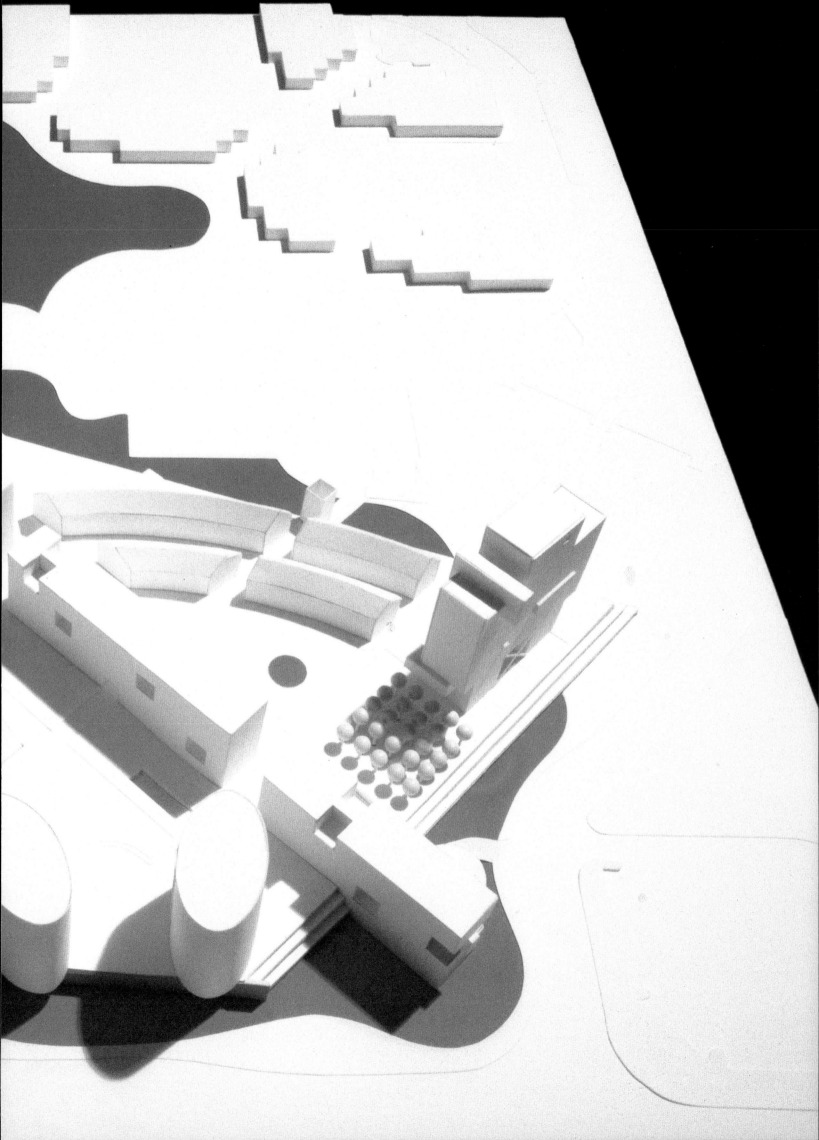

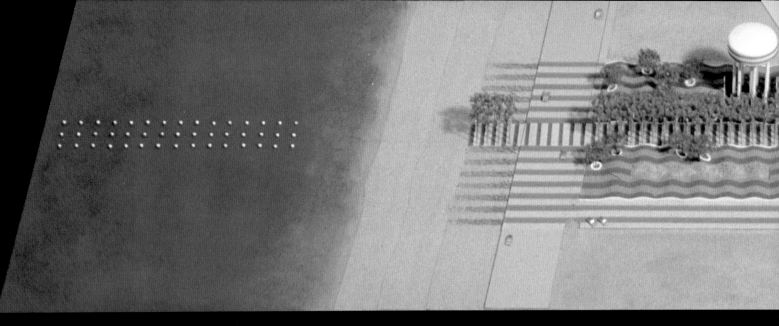

This project is a renovation and expansion of the swimming complex and museum on the Intracoastal Waterway in Fort Lauderdale. Once a public park is completed, the complex will stretch to the Atlantic Ocean as well.

The museum building is the front door to the complex. Filled with nautical imagery, it has a wave-shaped profile and clerestory windows shaped like kickboards, buoys, and starting blocks. This white volume is suspended over a series of supports constructed of coral rock, blue mosaic tile, yellow brick, blue-green reflective glass, red sandstone, and anodized aluminum. The building is raised off the ground to provide safety in case of flooding and to allow for views into the swimming complex beyond.

The complex includes competitive and diving pools as well as a training pool, a spa, and a children's pool. Behind the pools is a new multipurpose hall in the shape of a trapezoid intersected by a glass crescent lobby opening onto the waterway. The various elements of the Swimming Hall of Fame are connected by a wave-shaped walkway and by its landscape plan, a paving pattern in broad stripes running from the ocean to the waterway designed with landscape architect Martha Schwartz. The material of the stripes changes with the progression of the complex, from hedges and grass to concrete and asphalt.

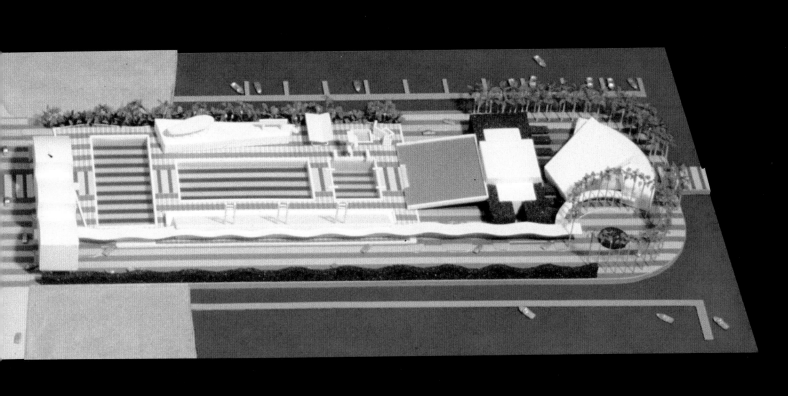

Washingtonian Center

Gaithersburg, Maryland
1987–90

This is a 230,000–square-foot shopping mall on a man-made lake in Washington, D.C. It includes eight movie theaters on the lower level and a health club on the top, as well as shops and four restaurants. The health club, with its indoor pool, sits atop the mall projecting over the lake. The shopping complex shares a parking garage with a nearby office building.

Two retail volumes flank a central open zone. A series of glass cylinders that contain more informal retail areas appear as large columns supporting a giant wedge. In silhouette this wedge form, the most prominent part of the structure, appears suspended in midair. The

east cylinder opens up to the space below and contains the elevator, escalators, and stairs. Along the water are a boardwalk and a terrace; the center's restaurants open onto this lakeside promenade.

The central volume is clad in glossy white metal panels, while the sides are in gray stucco. The facades at the ends have a series of windows in different shapes. The cylinders are covered in a checkerboard of frosted and clear glass.

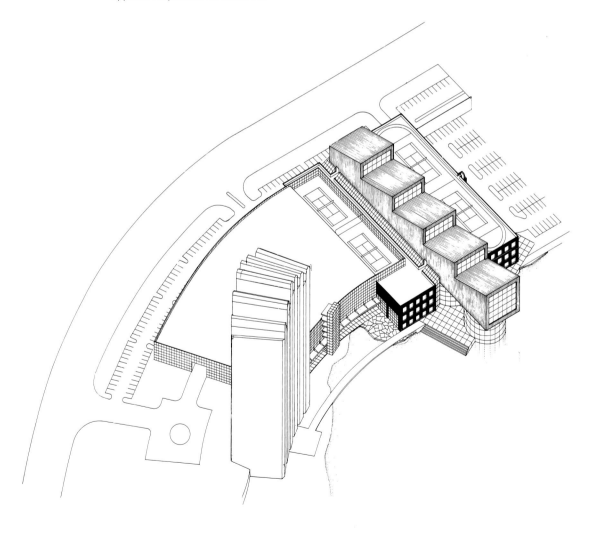

Below: Washingtonian Center is organized so that each floor is devoted to a specific use. Movie theaters are on the lowest level, and a health club is at the top. A series of cylindrical volumes leads pedestrians through the complex.

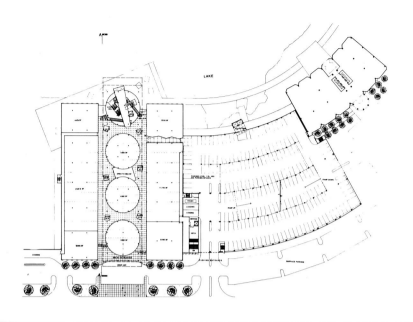

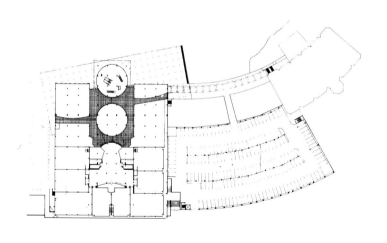

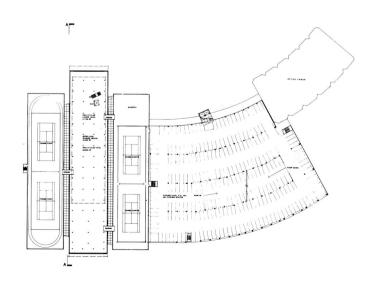

Hanna Winery

(Design proposal)
1988

This complex for a winery that produces 100,000 cases a year is sited on a knoll overlooking vineyards. Its components are separated to create a varied skyline like a medieval village surrounding a square. Actually a formal garden with four quadrants, the garden covers the caves for wine storage. Surrounding it are a series of freestanding structures. The form of each structure reflects its use: A wooden tower contains wine-tasting rooms, an apartment for the vintner, and an observation deck. A crescent-shaped administration building is clad in boulders. A corrugated metal and steel structure contains the tank farm. A blue-glazed block building houses the bottling plant, and a stucco shed was designed for equipment.

Three Palms

Jupiter, Florida
1988–90

This mixed-use development project includes a single story of retail space with a second-floor restaurant and a four-story office building. The L-shaped strip shopping center is distinguished by it overhang, which runs the length of the building and is punctured at regular intervals by palm trees. The office building is freestanding at the corner of the site. A trussed structure visually connects the retail and office buildings. In the office building this white steel framework is filled with a glass volume that serves as an atrium lobby and special offices. On the retail side the trusses break through the inner core of the building to create a courtyard.

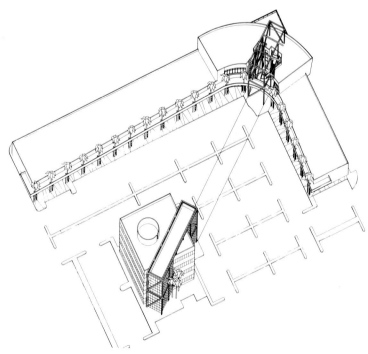

Yerba Buena Gardens Office Building

(Competition entry)
1988

This 500,000–square-foot office building for San Francisco's South of Market district is designed for a corner lot occupied by a dilapidated building with a historic facade. Arquitectonica chose to demolish the building but preserve its facade. The facade was to be incorporated into the new building as one element of a collage. The old yellow terra-cotta wall would float in front of a gray slate and gray glass volume that also serves as a base for an office tower of green glass and steel. The slate and glass are arranged to form a giant brick coursing pattern with the slate as "bricks" and the glass as "mortar"—all in contrast to the mustard yellow of the terra-cotta.

The gray base, related in height to the other buildings in the neighborhood, is punctured by a huge vertical opening marking the lobby entrance. On the side street the building is given a second facade, designed as a four-story granite grid relating in scale and color to adjacent brick buildings.

The tower is framed by a multi-story, exposed stainless steel grid with cross cables that relate to the bridge structures in the distance. A white marble prow with bay windows tops the composition.

The office tower shifts slightly off the base and rises above it. At the top, the building's prow—a nautical allusion—looks out toward San Francisco Bay.

Bank of America

Beverly Hills, California
1988–91

This low-slung, three-story office building takes up the width of a full block of Wilshire Boulevard and backs up to the playing fields of the Horace Mann School. It rests on an L-shaped three-story underground parking garage that accommodates 430 cars.

The structure is broken down into two large volumes that share a three-story atrium but seem to slip past each other. The smaller of the two volumes, which faces west, wraps around the corner of Wilshire and Robertson boulevards as a large-scale green metal grid with green glass. The scaleless wall appears as a giant Cinerama screen set against the backdrop of hills. At the corner a piece of the first and second floors has been carved out to reveal the curved glass entrance to the Bank of America. The third floor cantilevers out above.

Along Wilshire Boulevard the larger volume is a curved black wall of alternating bands of granite and glass. A white marble balcony appears as an abstract stripe over a row of tall, slender palm trees. In a reference to film, the east (Arnaz Drive) facade has alternating bands of black and silver glass.

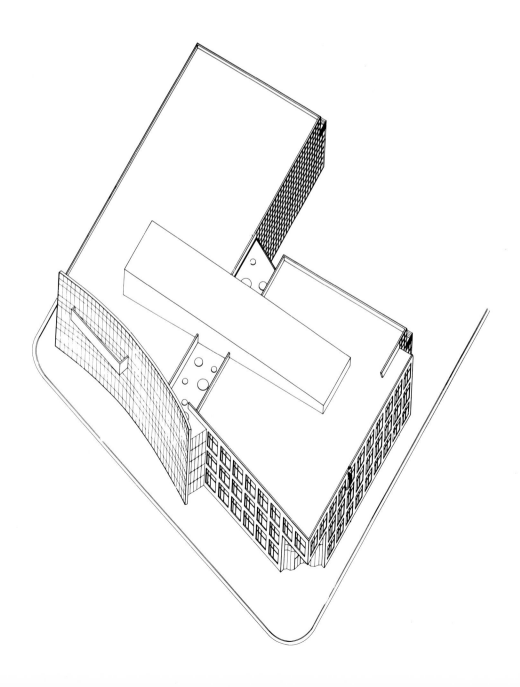

A variety of shapes and building materials are juxtaposed in unexpected ways in Arquitectonica's Bank of America. The complex's various volumes are linked together both structurally and visually, and the building seems to tilt over the plaza.

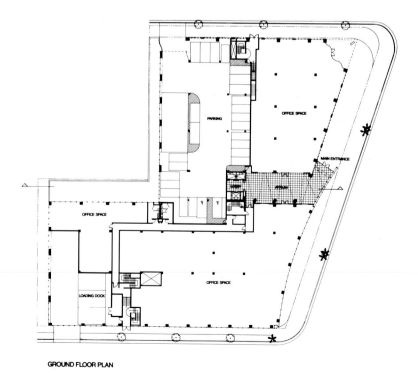

GROUND FLOOR PLAN

*Opposite: On one side of the Wilshire
Boulevard facade a balcony is
suspended over the sidewalk level.*

*Above: The other facade, the smaller of
the two volumes, is treated differently;
a piece of it is cut away to reveal the
interior. The third floor is cantilevered
over this abstract opening.*

Commercial Place

Fort Lauderdale, Florida
1988-90

This structure consists of twin four-story office buildings set at an angle to each other and placed 45 degrees off the street to create two triangular courts. The first of these, a large palm court, serves as an automobile drop-off area and as a ceremonial entrance to the buildings. A second, shaded court functions as an outdoor dining area.

The complex, which houses primarily multiple-tenant offices, also has a health club, a conference center, and a restaurant.

The reinforced concrete buildings are clad in synthetic painted stucco and reflective blue glass.

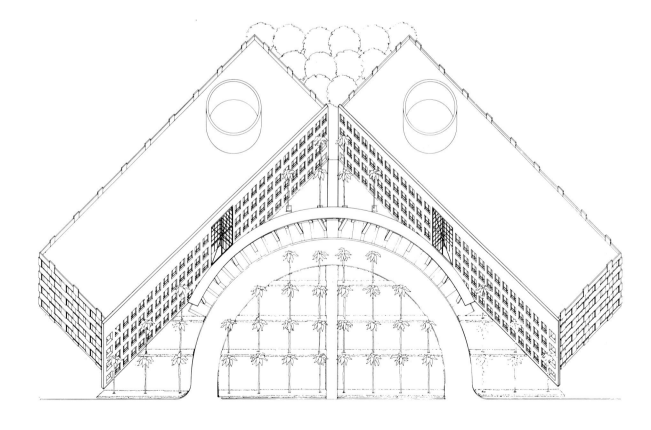

U.S. Pavilion, Seville Expo '92

(Competition entry)
1989

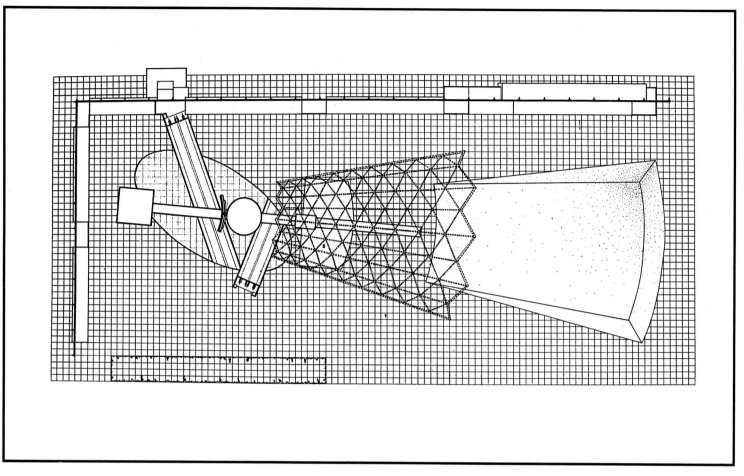

This entry in the design competition for the U.S. Pavilion at the 1992 World's Fair in Seville expresses the relationship between humankind, contemporary technology, and the earth's natural resources. The design seeks a new balance between man-made systems and the preservation of environment and culture. Thus, the anti-building creates an open space; the building itself is placed almost entirely underground to give the exhibition space maximum flexibility in one level and to allow the outdoor plaza to make a more poetic statement.

The pavilion is designed as a collage of geometric forms that rise out of the open space. "The Ocean" is a reflecting pool, a thin skin of water that would cover the ground plane and become kinetic with personal interaction. "The New Continent," a trapezoidal form, is actually the roof of the auditorium. Rather than the more expected glass pyramid, it is intended to be covered with wildflowers and turf. "Reaching to the Sky," a stainless steel diffraction tower and a

sculpture prism by day, would become a laser light sculpture at night. A performance stage cantilevers out from a tower. A single giant spectravision screen atop the performance stage tower would project both images and information.

At the entry ramp a blue perforated metal "People Wall" symbolizes America's multiethnic composition; the entry procession then leads to an escalator ride down a translucent tube with holographically generated prismatic colors.

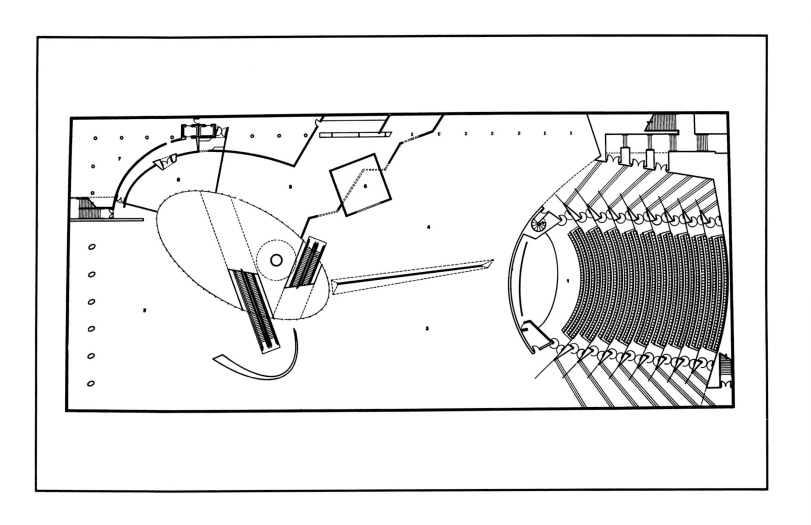

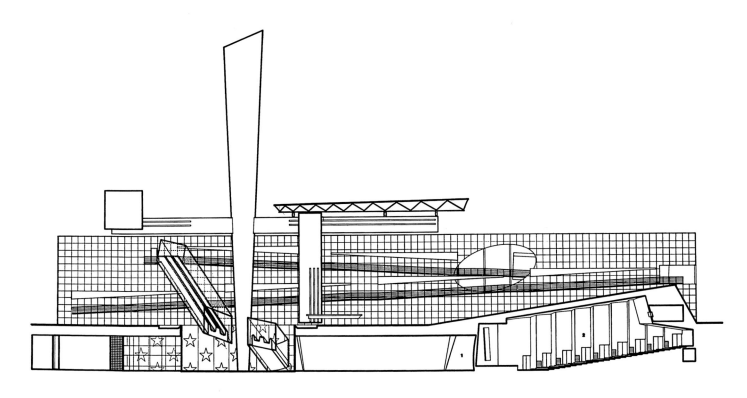

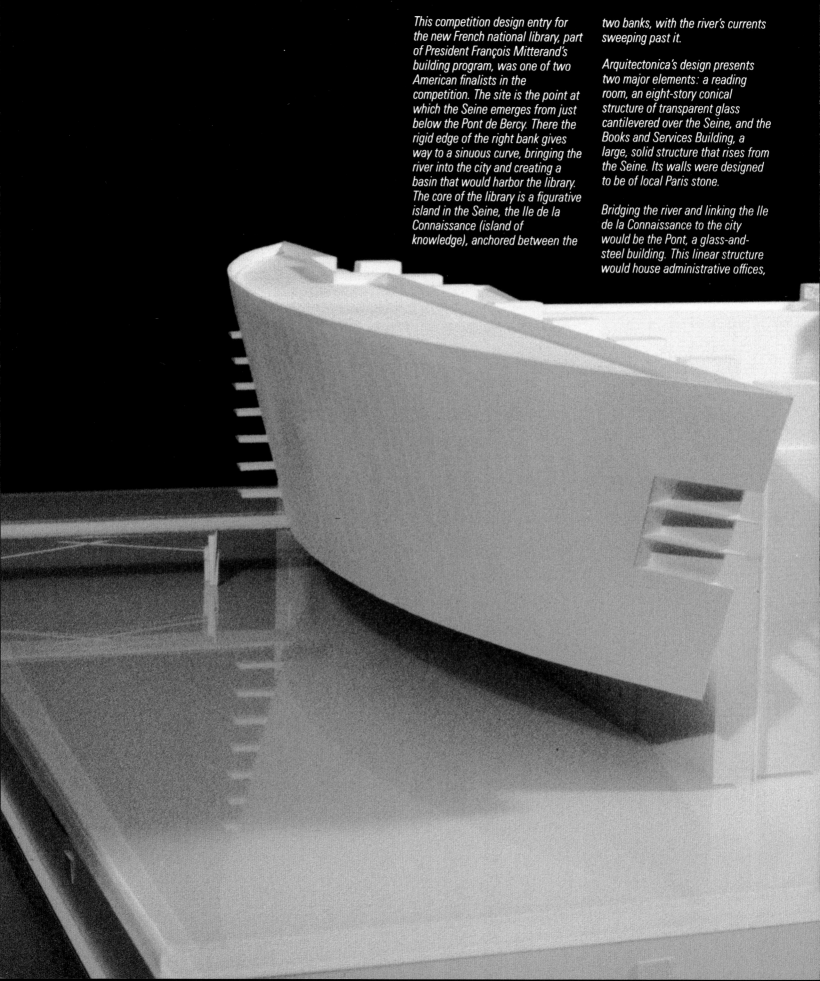

This competition design entry for the new French national library, part of President François Mitterand's building program, was one of two American finalists in the competition. The site is the point at which the Seine emerges from just below the Pont de Bercy. There the rigid edge of the right bank gives way to a sinuous curve, bringing the river into the city and creating a basin that would harbor the library. The core of the library is a figurative island in the Seine, the Ile de la Connaissance (island of knowledge), anchored between the two banks, with the river's currents sweeping past it.

Arquitectonica's design presents two major elements: a reading room, an eight-story conical structure of transparent glass cantilevered over the Seine, and the Books and Services Building, a large, solid structure that rises from the Seine. Its walls were designed to be of local Paris stone.

Bridging the river and linking the Ile de la Connaissance to the city would be the Pont, a glass-and-steel building. This linear structure would house administrative offices, galleries, shops, and the main entrance to the library. The Pont would sit on the elevated Place de la Bibliothèque spanning the upper and lower quays.

Trees would grow on the Place de la Bibliothèque, forming a grove rising from a patterned field of stone, low vegetation, and water. A monumental stairway would link the upper quay and the plaza; the stairway would have elements of both traditional and water sculpture. The plaza continues across the street to create a large urban park bisected by a new boulevard, the Voie Nouvelle.

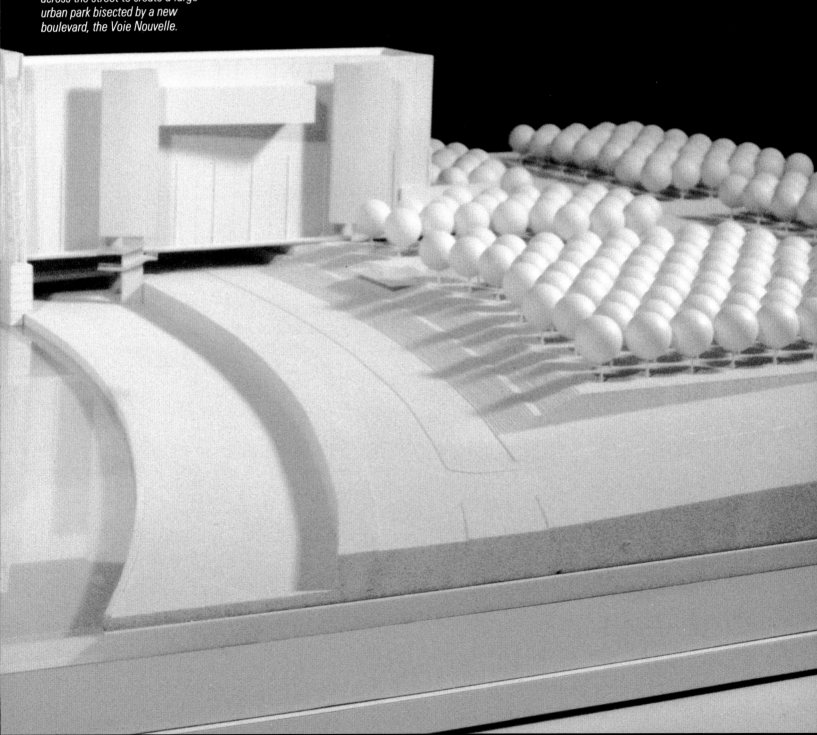

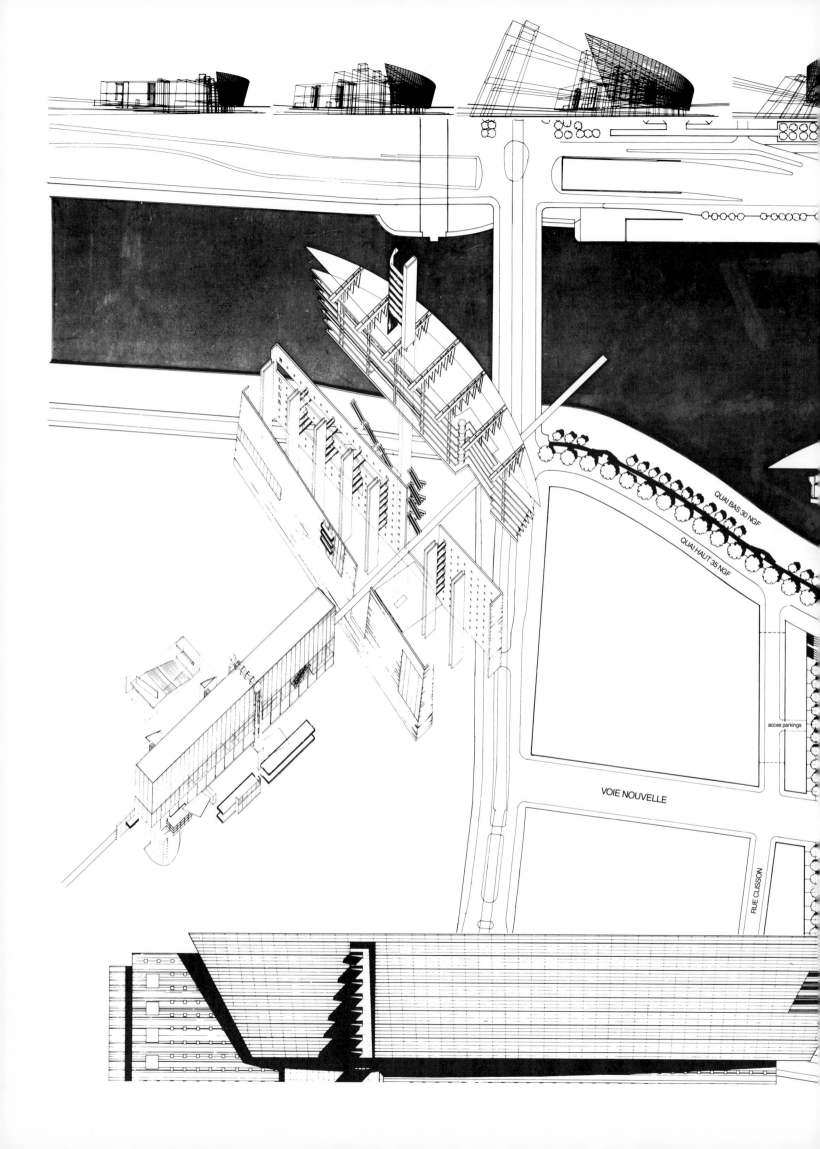

QUAI BAS 30 NGF

QUAI HAUT 35 NGF

acces parkings

VOIE NOUVELLE

RUE CLISSON

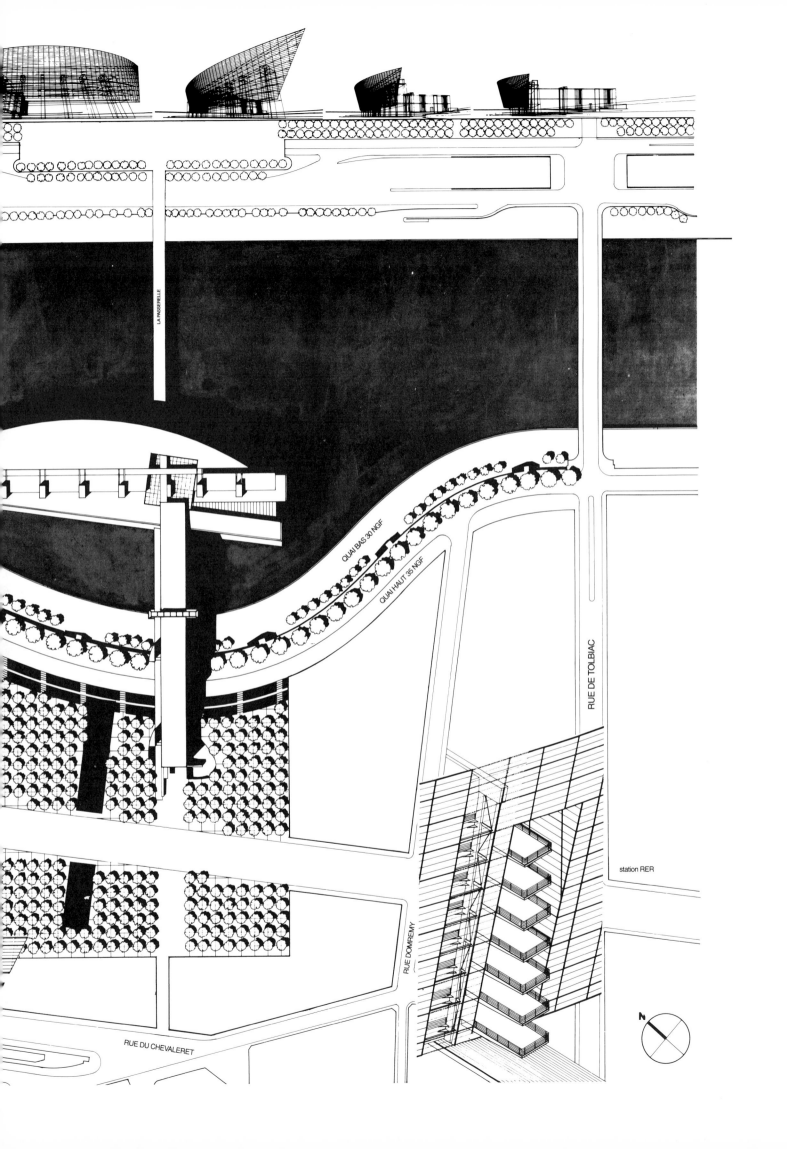

LA PASSERELLE

QUAI BAS 30 NGF

QUAI HAUT 35 NGF

RUE DE TOLBIAC

RUE DOMRÉMY

station RER

RUE DU CHEVALERET

N

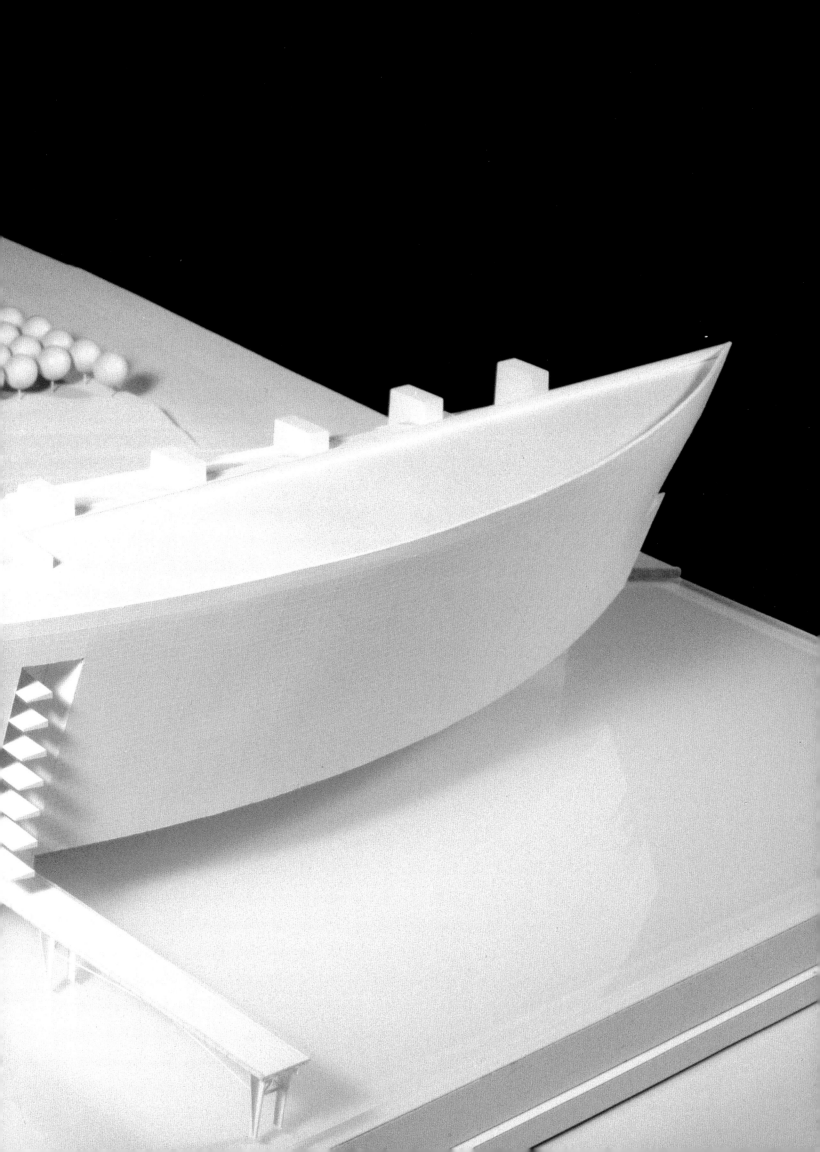

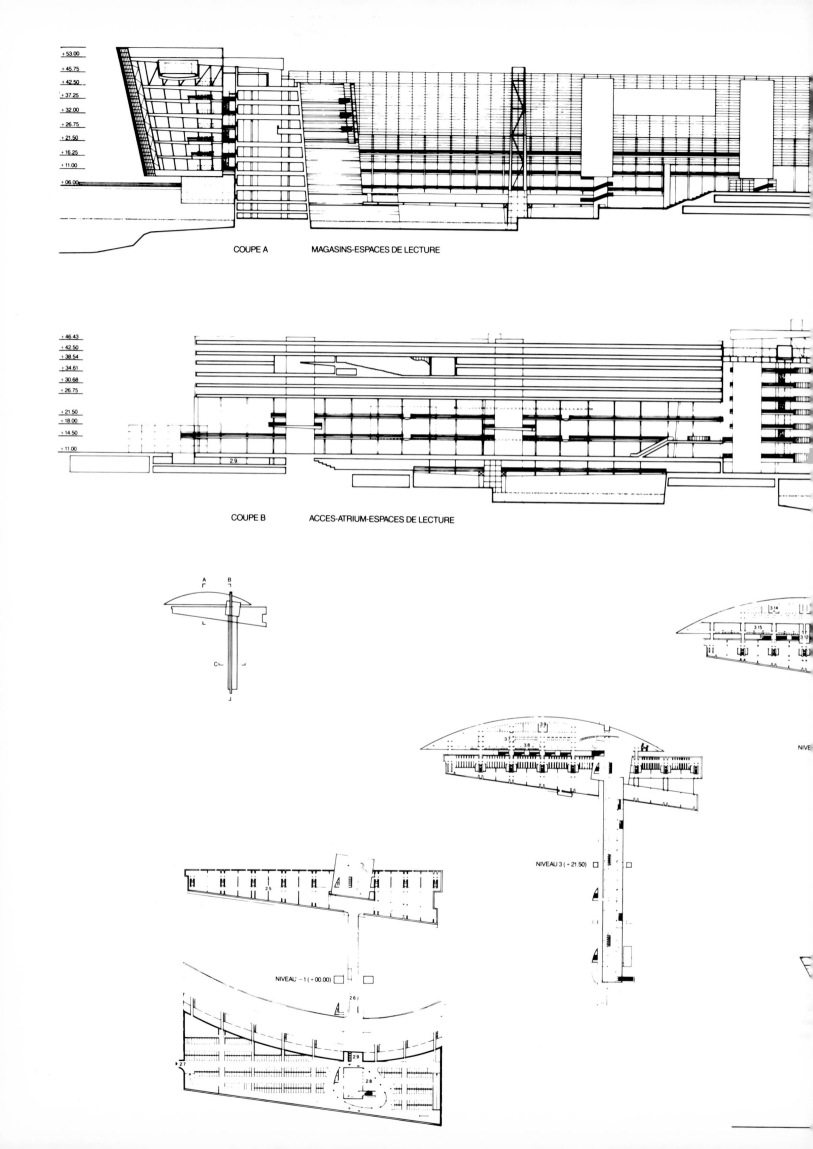

+ 53.00
+ 45.75
+ 42.50
+ 37.25
+ 32.00
+ 26.75
+ 21.50
+ 16.25
+ 11.00
+ 06.00

COUPE A   MAGASINS-ESPACES DE LECTURE

+ 46.43
+ 42.50
+ 38.54
+ 34.61
+ 30.68
+ 26.75

+ 21.50
+ 18.00
+ 14.50

+ 11.00

2 9

COUPE B   ACCES-ATRIUM-ESPACES DE LECTURE

A B

C

3 14
3 15 3 12

NIVE

3 9
3 7 3 8

NIVEAU 3 (+ 21.50)

2 5

NIVEAU – 1 (+ 00.00)

2 6

2 9

2 7

2 8

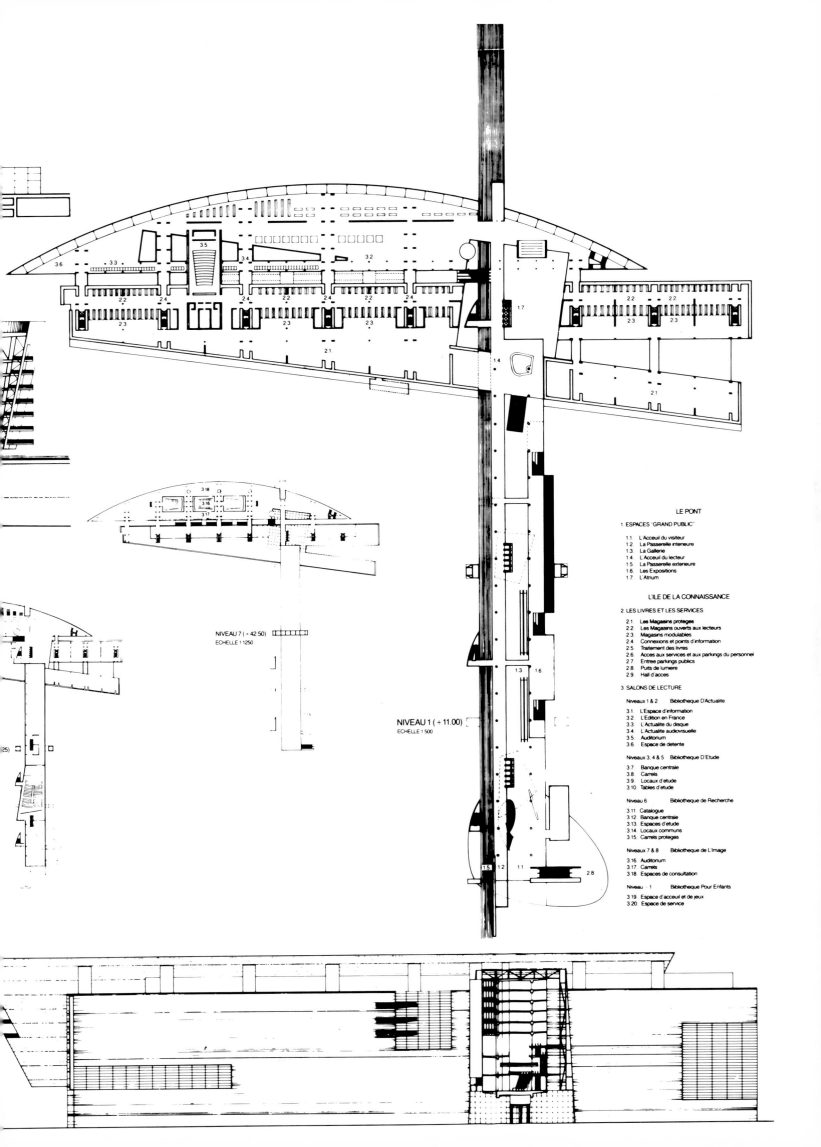

LE PONT

1 ESPACES "GRAND PUBLIC"

1.1 L'Acceuil du visiteur
1.2 La Passerelle interieure
1.3 La Gallerie
1.4 L'Acceuil du lecteur
1.5 La Passerelle exterieure
1.6 Les Expositions
1.7 L'Atrium

L'ILE DE LA CONNAISSANCE

2 LES LIVRES ET LES SERVICES

2.1 Les Magasins proteges
2.2 Les Magasins ouverts aux lecteurs
2.3 Magasins modulables
2.4 Connexions et ponts d'information
2.5 Traitement des livres
2.6 Acces aux services et aux parkings du personnel
2.7 Entree parkings publics
2.8 Puits de lumiere
2.9 Hall d'acces

3 SALONS DE LECTURE

Niveaux 1 & 2   Bibliotheque D'Actualite

3.1 L'Espace d'information
3.2 L'Edition en France
3.3 L'Actualite du disque
3.4 L'Actualite audiovisuelle
3.5 Auditorium
3.6 Espace de detente

Niveaux 3, 4 & 5   Bibliotheque D'Etude

3.7 Banque centrale
3.8 Carrels
3.9 Locaux d'etude
3.10 Tables d'etude

Niveau 6   Bibliotheque de Recherche

3.11 Catalogue
3.12 Banque centrale
3.13 Espaces d'etude
3.14 Locaux communs
3.15 Carrels proteges

Niveaux 7 & 8   Bibliotheque de L'Image

3.16 Auditorium
3.17 Carrels
3.18 Espaces de consultation

Niveau -1   Bibliotheque Pour Enfants

3.19 Espace d'acceuil et de jeux
3.20 Espace de service

NIVEAU 7 (+ 42.50)
ECHELLE 1:1250

NIVEAU 1 (+ 11.00)
ECHELLE 1:500

Banque de Luxembourg

G. D. Luxembourg
1989

This new headquarters for the Banque de Luxembourg sits at the focus of the Boulevard Royale in the business center of the city. Most of the building's space—200,000 square feet—is allotted to eight underground levels used for parking and for safes. The six-story aboveground building houses the executive offices, boardroom, conference centers, and public banking lobby. Designed as intersecting glass-, marble-, and granite-clad forms, it is a corner building sited just where the Boulevard Royale makes a sharp turn—thus setting up the axial relationship of the building to the street. In turn, the vistas from the bank headquarters look down the boulevard and over the rooftops of historic houses to the Parc Prince Henri.

The parallelogram-shaped central core of the building, clad in polished black granite and matching dark-tinted glass, is intended to emerge from the middle of the architectural composition as both background and anchor. A second, rectangular volume, clad in chassagne with matching amber-tinted glass, intersects the core suspended above the ground. Although from the front it appears to be cantilevered, it is in fact supported from the rear by a series of elliptical gray granite columns and in the front by a monumental granite block. This huge, rough-hewn block is to have the name and

logo of the bank chiseled on it.

A third volume emerges from the other two, reaching out toward the plaza and the corner. This volume is more sculptural, a segment of a reverse elliptical cone, and its curving facade faces the corner. It is clad entirely in lightly tinted glass that is supported by radiating stainless steel mullions in a vertical pattern. Housed in this third volume are the building's public and ceremonial spaces; its light, almost transparent nature is intended as a contrast to the solidity of the other volumes. The curvilinear shape of the third volume is meant as a gesture to the city, introducing a new form of artistic expression to the urban landscape and setting the structure apart from the more rectangular forms of nearby buildings.

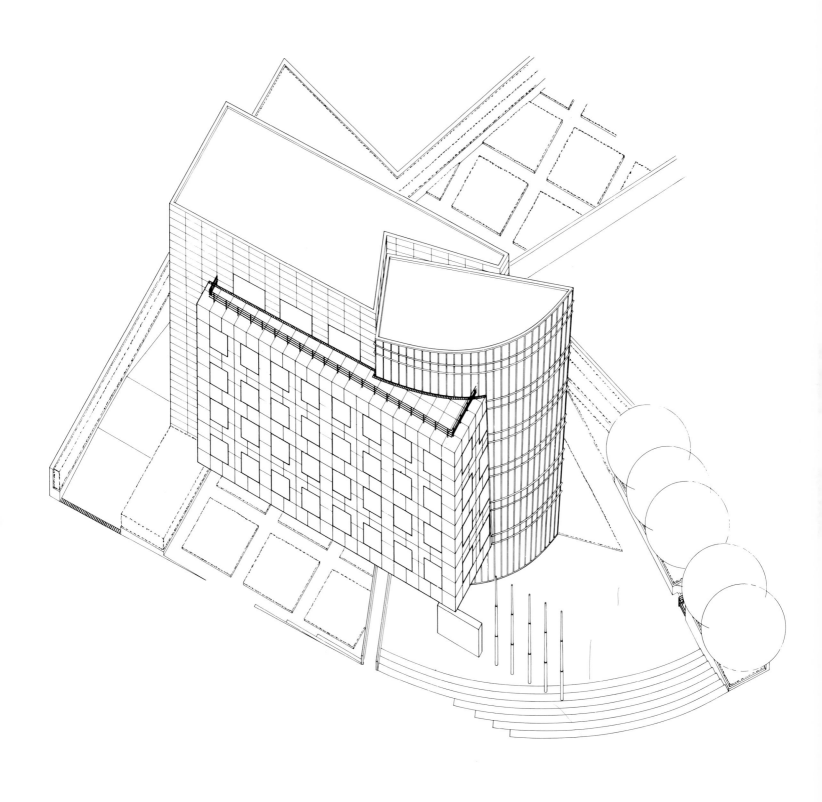

Amir House

**Beverly Hills, California
1989**

The Amir residence was conceived as a study in intersecting planes and volumes, and a stairway slides in among them. A major design element makes up the major living space, a glass volume that curves on one side and angles on the other. Functionally, the house has five bedrooms, a tennis court, and a cabana area.

The composition is abstract, and yet almost baroque. In plan the house has cubist dimensions, but the execution is far more romantic than geometric. The rooms are shaped by the intersections of forms and volumes. The walls are fluid; only the main square is rigid.

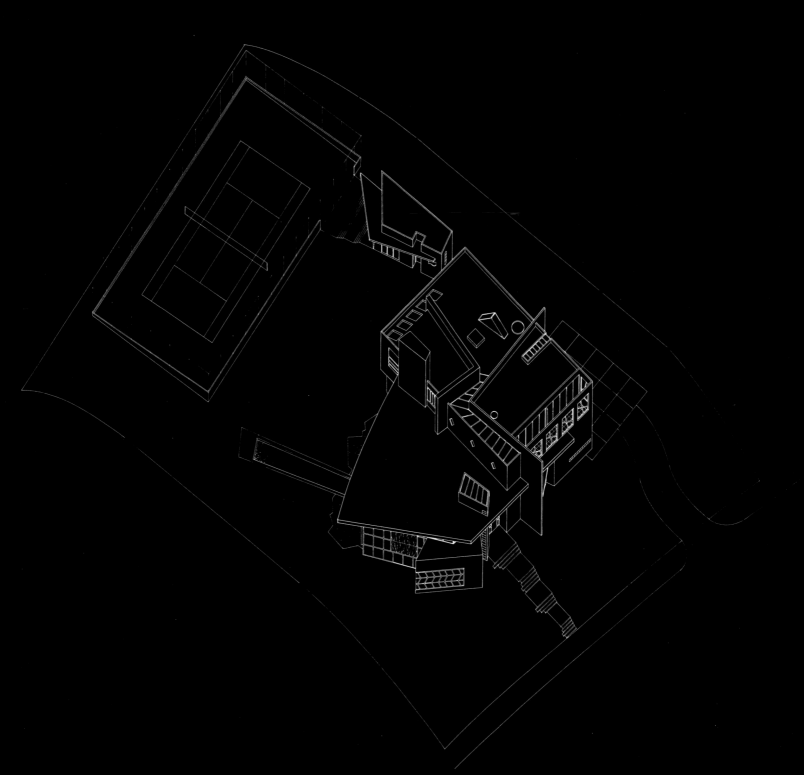

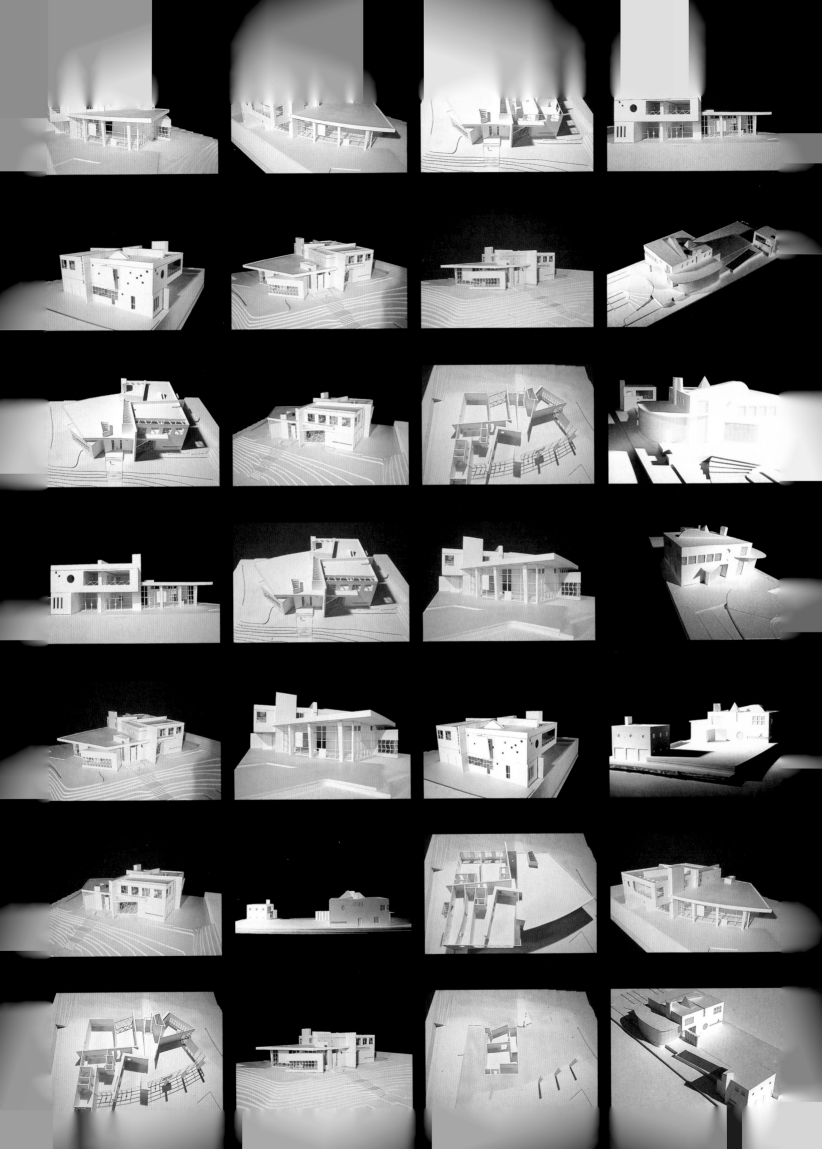

Arbed Headquarters

(Competition entry)
1989

In this design competition entry for a new headquarters for Arbed, a major European steel company, Arquitectonica chose to explore the possibilities of raw steel for both its structural uses and its aesthetic possibilities—to make it into an "expressive" architectural element. The site, in Luxembourg, Belgium, was partially occupied by a lake, and the proposed building sought to link two sides of this with steel trusses. Each truss was given a unique architectural identity—an ellipse, a curve, and a V-shape. The trusses, in turn, allowed the creation of both clear-span and cantilevered spaces.

Private Residence

**Hillsborough Beach, Florida
1989**

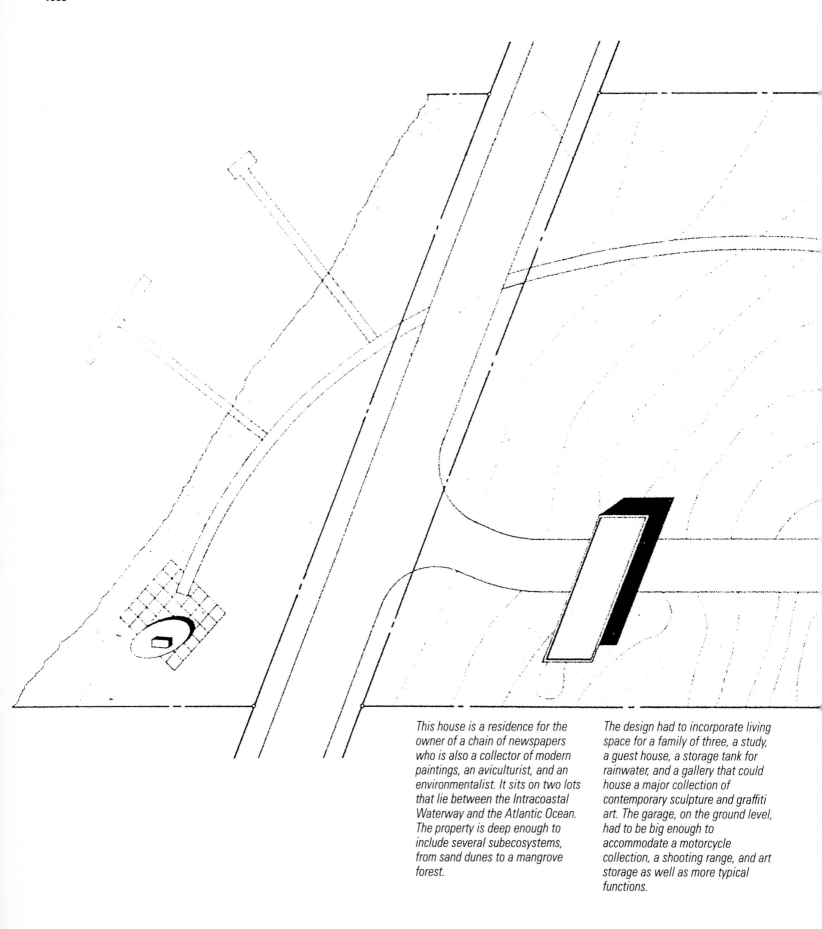

This house is a residence for the owner of a chain of newspapers who is also a collector of modern paintings, an aviculturist, and an environmentalist. It sits on two lots that lie between the Intracoastal Waterway and the Atlantic Ocean. The property is deep enough to include several subecosystems, from sand dunes to a mangrove forest.

The design had to incorporate living space for a family of three, a study, a guest house, a storage tank for rainwater, and a gallery that could house a major collection of contemporary sculpture and graffiti art. The garage, on the ground level, had to be big enough to accommodate a motorcycle collection, a shooting range, and art storage as well as more typical functions.

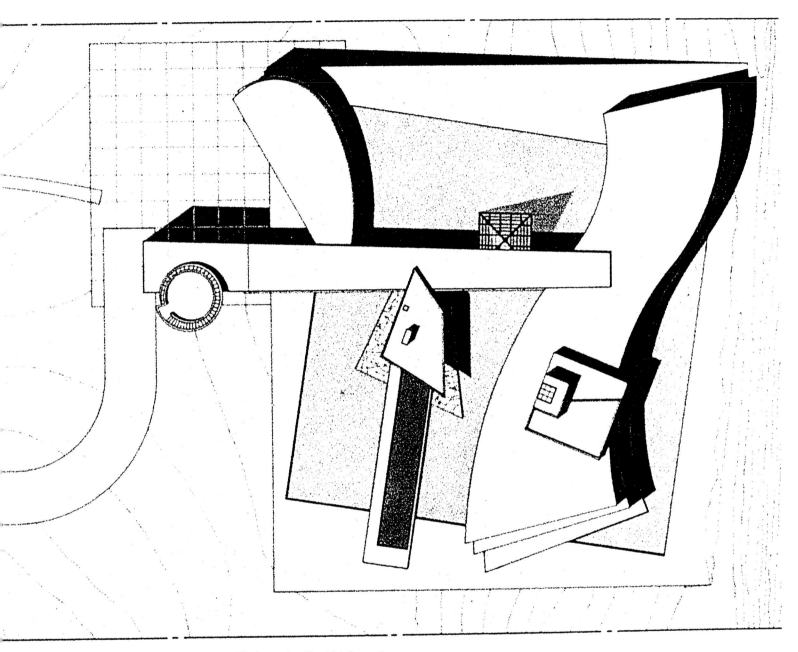

The house has a swimming pool, naturally aerated so that fish will swim in it, and a huge bird cage for exotic species.

The various volumes are linked by a gallery reached from a spiral staircase that goes through the cone of the water tank and emerges from it to create an observation deck. Another stair pierces the trapezoid-shaped study, suspended over the water and connected to the house by a catwalk.

The house itself, which faces the beach, is a wave-like structure—in fact, a series of sliding horizontal planes. Inside, the rooms are formed by freestanding planes and volumes that serve as dividers to create spaces.

In plan this private residence sits on a platform in the shape of a perfect square. On top of it rotates a second square, which contains the natural swimming pool.

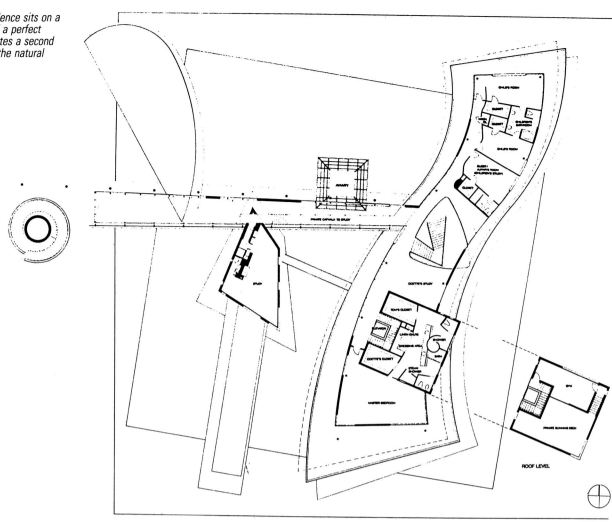

A big funnel-shaped corridor angles slightly as it leads through the house. A chlorinated lap pool bridges the natural pool.

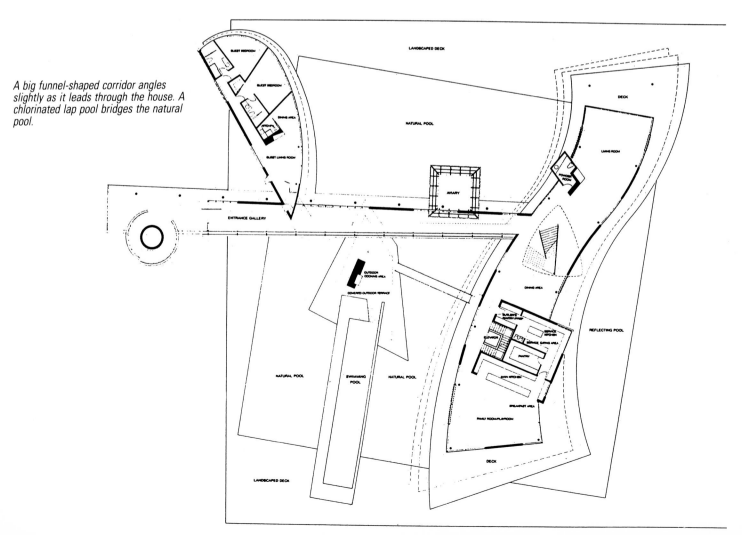

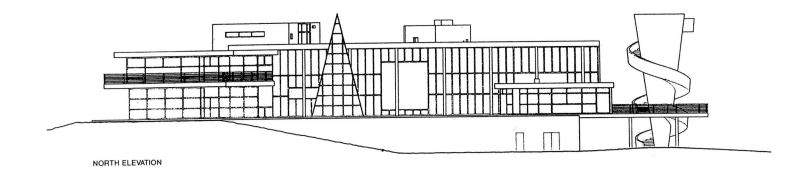

NORTH ELEVATION

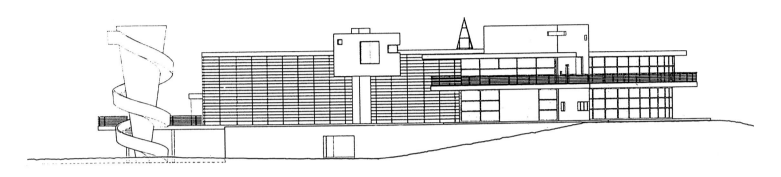

SOUTH ELEVATION

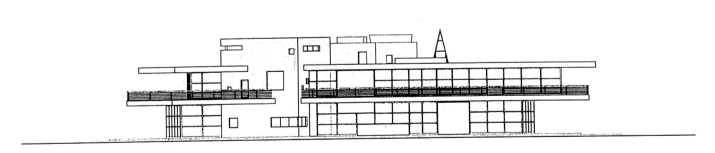

EAST ELEVATION

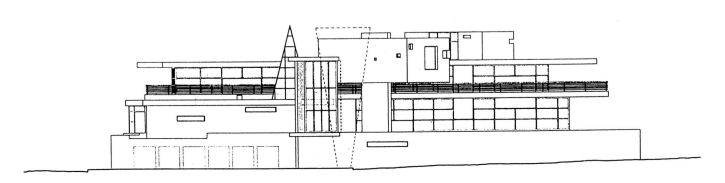

WEST ELEVATION

House in Coconut Grove

Coconut Grove, Florida
1987–89

Arquitectonica's principals designed this house in the Coconut Grove area of Miami as their own residence: by their description not an architect's house, but "a house for a family." The house is a rectangular box in three levels. The lower level is below the floodplain and contains garages, storage space, and a large children's playroom. The main level, or piano nobile, contains the public rooms and a guest bedroom. The upper level has the family's bedrooms.

The exterior of the house is gray-green stucco with white trim, but despite its plain shape and subdued palette the house is not austere. Punched windows with varied detail form a checkerboard arrangement: Bright blue semicircular and triangular overhangs, appropriate for the climate, cast shadows of varying shapes. Shutters and window boxes, clear and frosted panes, glass block, and tile make each window a different composition.

Inside, the windows frame a sequence of views, and asymmetrically placed walls, like sliding planes, define an informal plan. Details include reminders of locale: tropical fish swim on the frosted glass of the front door, pictorial tiles designed from vintage postcard scenes of Florida serve as wainscots in the bathrooms, and single-piece cypress trunks stripped by Micosukees form the stair handrails.

Bibliography

1975

Progressive Architecture, January 1975, "The 22nd P/A Awards Award: A House on the Waterfront in Florida [Spear House]," pp. 46–47.

1978

Progressive Architecture, January 1978, "The 25th P/A Awards—Citation: Architectural Design—Arquitectonica for The Babylon," p. 83.

AMACADEMY, The Newsletter of the American Academy in Rome, June 1978, "Fellows 1978–79: Laurinda Hope Spear," pp. 12–13.

Miami Herald-Neighbors Magazine, April 2, 1978, "Neighbors See Red over Pink House," by Jeff Birnbaum, p. 1.

Miami Herald-Neighbors Magazine, December 28, 1978, "Pink House in Shores is Ready for Owners," by Jonathan D. Salant, p. 3.

1979

Skyline, March 1979, "Helmsley Hires Arquitectonica," p. 12.

House Beautiful, May 1979, "Color Defines Contemporary Structure," by Susan Grant Lewin, p. 180.

Vogue, June 1979, "What Counts," by Lorraine Davis, pp. 186–87, 241–44.

Architectural Design, July 9, 1979, "Buildings in AD—Arquitectonica," pp. 186–89.

Miami News, July 25, 1979, "Boom Rises Higher/Condo [The Palace] to Tower 41 Stories," by Larry Birger.

Miami Herald-Business News, July 26, 1979, "Brickell Highrise [The Palace] Goes Up," by Mike Clary and Steve Sidlo, pp. 1–2.

New York Times Magazine-HOME Magazine, September 30, 1979, "The Power of Color [Spear House]," by Marilyn Bethany, pp. 18–23.

House Beautiful, October 1979, "Color Blazes a Trail," by Susan Grant Lewin, pp. 158–63, 250–53.

Progressive Architecture, December 1979, "Layers of Meaning," by John Morris Dixon, pp. 66–71.

1980

Young Architects, Yale School of Architecture, January 1980, "Arquitectonica," by George Ranalli, p. 2.

Progressive Architecture, January 1980, "The 27th P/A Awards—Citation, Architectural Design—Arquitectonica for The Atlantis," p. 109.

Toronto Globe & Mail, April 10, 1980, "Flamboyant Miami Architects," by Susan Doubilet.

GQ/Gentleman's Quarterly, February 1980, "The Greatest of Ease [Spear House]," pp. 98–109.

Penton/IPC Review, vol. 5, no. 1 (Quarter I, 1980), "Progressive Architecture Honors Architectural Innovators."

Miami Herald, March 2, 1980, "Planned Surrealistic Condo Gets Design Award for Excellence," p. 35H.

Vogue, April 1980, "Legs, Legs, Legs [Spear House]," pp. 220–27.

Real Estate Digest—Miami, Spring/ Summer 1980, "Ultra-Luxury Condominiums—The Atlantis, The Imperial, The Palace, The Gemini," pp. 34–54.

Progressive Architecture, August 1980, "Miami Downtown—Endless Wave?" and "Arquitectonica on Brickell," by Suzanne Stephens, pp. 52–59.

Residential Interiors, September/ October 1980, "Miami Modern/ Arquitectonica Creates an Urban Sensibility in a Suburban Setting," by John Duka, pp. 80–83.

House Beautiful's Building Manual, Fall 1980, "Color in Architecture," by Susan Grant Lewin, p. 72, and "New Dimension for Form and Function," pp. 73–77, cover.

Progressive Architecture, December 1980, "In Progress: The Overseas Tower, Miami, Florida," p. 40.

1981

Architectural Record, January 1981, "Suburban Renewal," p. 80.

Domus (Italy), January 1981, no. 613, "The Dream of a House," by Fulvio Irace, pp. 11–15.

Life, March 1981, "Living Color: Today's Architects Paint the Town Red. And Pink. And . . . ," pp. 62–65.

A+U, "American Architecture, After Modernism," March 1981 Extra Edition, Chapter 9—"Work of Arquitectonica Group," pp. 183–202, guest edited by Robert A. M. Stern.

House and Garden, March 1982, "Women in Architecture: Breaking New Ground," by Suzanne Stephens, pp. 146–49.

GA/Global Architecture Houses 8, May 1981, "New Waves in American Architecture, Arquitectonica International Corporation," pp. 98–113, cover.

Miami Herald—Business, July 20, 1981, "Coral Gables 'Kids' Make Their Mark at Arquitectonica," by Larry Birger, p. 5.

Art in America, Summer 1981, "Harbingers: Ten Architects," by Martin Filler, pp. 114–23.

AIA Journal, September 1981, "Journal's Photo Contest [Spear House]," p. 58.

Iowa Architect, September/October 1981, "Iowa Chapter of the American Institute of Architects 1981 Convention— [Work of] Arquitectonica," p. 58.

Miami News, October 16, 1981, "The Architecture of the Future—Miami in the Making," by Jayne Merkel, pp. 1B, 4B.

New York Times, November 12, 1981, "My Son, the Architect: Houses for Parents," by Joan Kron, pp. C1, C6.

1982

Perspecta 18, 1982, "Portfolio of Recent Works—Arquitectonica," pp. 171–79.

Decoracion de Vanidades III, 1982 special edition, "La Casa de una Arquitecta," pp. 112–15.

Miami Herald, April 4, 1982, "Out of the Blue—Arquitectonica Turns Design into Child's Play," by Beth Dunlop, pp. 1, 8.

Wall Street Journal, May 20, 1982, "Bustling Town Builders, Banks, Ports Thrive in Miami as City becomes Trade Center," by L. Erik Calonius, pp. 1, 20.

Design Review, June 1982, "Emerging Voices, Arquitectonica," by Richard Oliver, p. 9, cover.

GQ/ Gentleman's Quarterly, June 1982, "Design's New Spectrum," by Peter Carlsen, pp. 163–65.

Progressive Architecture, July 1982, "Peeping into Pandora's Box, The Place—Miami, Florida," pp. 82–87.

House Beautiful, July 1982, "Great Kitchens, Socko Colors Add Playfulness to this New Kitchen/Family Room of a 1918 Florida House," by Susan Grant Lewin, pp. 46–49.

Decoration Internationale (Italy), July/ August 1982, "The Spear House," photograph by Donatella Brun, p. 1, cover.

Architectural Record, August 1982, "Making it in Miami," by Charles K. Gandee, pp. 112–22.

National Geographic, August 1982, "FLORIDA—A Time for Reckoning," by William S. Ellis," pp. 172–217.

SD/Space Design—A Monthly Journal of Art & Architecture, August 1982, no. 215, "Urban Contexts, Arquitectonica," p. 126.

New York Times—The HOME Section, September 16, 1982, "Design Notebook, Emerging Young Architects— Diversity and New Directions," by Paul Goldberger, pp. C1, C6.

Florida Architect—Journal of the Florida Chapter of the American Institute of Architects, Fall 1982, "1982 FA/AIA Awards for Excellence in Architecture" and "A Most Extravagant Core of Glass Wall [Overseas Tower].." by Charles Gwathmey," p. 11.

Corporate Design, September/October 1982, "Overseas Builds to be Remembered," pp. 46–51, cover.

Residential Interiors, September/ October 1982, "Miami Modern/ Arquitectonica Creates an Urban Sensibility in a Suburban Setting," pp. 80–83.

Architectural Digest, October 1982, "Architecture: Houses of the Future," by Paul Goldberger, pp. 162–69.

OICA—Semanario de Actualidad (Peru), November 8, 1982, "Personas: Limeno Fort revoluciona con color el rascacielos," pp. 40–41.

Independent Professional, November 1982, "Designing and Building Florida," pp. 2, 19.

Newsweek, November 8, 1982, "The Sky's the Limit—Free Spirits," by Douglas Davis and Maggie Malone, pp. 66–76.

International Herald Tribune, December 4, 1982, "North American Real Estate," pp. 7–9.

1983

Miami Herald, January 15, 1983, "Bold Towering Center Proves Sky's the Limit," by Beth Dunlop, p. 3B.

Progressive Architecture, February 1983, "Rich and Famous," by Pilar Viladas, pp. 99–197, cover.

At Home with Architecture, "Contemporary Views of the House," February 10, 1983, "Spear House, Miami, Florida, 1977," pp. 10–11, and "Maba House, Houston, Texas, 1981," pp. 12–13.

San Diego Union, February 27, 1983, "Futuristic Home Designers Hollering, 'Anything Goes,'" by Roger Shawley, p. F1.

Florida Trend, March 1983, "Arquitectonica: Designs for Living that Shake People Up," by Annetta Miller, pp. 36–40.

United—The Magazine of the Friendly Skies, March 1983, "Making It in Miami: Two Young Florida Architects are Merging Marriage, Business, and Careers that are Rising as Fast as the Bold, New Buildings They Design," by Patricia Roberts, pp. 71–76.

Diario las Americas, March 12, 1983, "The Helmsley Center Will Be the Colossus of Miami," p. 44H.

Miami Herald, March 13, 1983, "Fort-Brescia Featured Speaker at The Flagler Museum," p. 44H.

CLIC (Sweden), Spring 1983, "The New Skyscrapers," by Bobo Karlsson, pp. 180–85.

Florida Architect, Spring 1983, "Awards Program Dazzle in Mid-Florida and Florida South," pp. 16–17.

Diario Las Americas, April 3, 1983, "Soho Fashion Center in New York," by Enrique Llaca, p. 8D.

Miami Review and Daily Record, April 7, 1983, "Horizon Hill Center," by Lesa Richman, pp. 1–5.

Diario Las Americas, April 23, 1983, "Horizon Hill Center," by Enrique Llaca, p. 9B.

Christian Science Monitor, April 29, 1983, "Architecture in Pursuit of Extremism," by Jany Holtz Kay, p. 9.

Miami Herald, May 1, 1983, "People: Fort-Brescia Guest Speaker at International Convention of the Building Owners and Managers Association," p. 26H.

House and Garden, June 1983, "High-Rise Hotshots," by Martin Filler, pp. 120–29.

Architectural Record, July 1983, "Once Again—Primary Colors," pp. 92–95, cover.

Wall Street Journal, July 7, 1983, "Architectural Firm Alters Miami's Skyline and Calls Attention to Its Designs," by L. Erik Calonius, Section 2, p. 1.

Miami Herald—Tropic Magazine, July 31, 1983, "The Sky's the Limit," by John Dorschner, pp. 10–16, cover.

Brutus (Japan), August 1, 1980, no. 70, "Neo Y Chromosome," by Tetsu Fukaya, pp. 144–45.

GA/Global Architecture Document 7, August 1983, "GA Interview: Arquitectonica," pp. 4–12, "GA Document: The Imperial, The Atlantis, The Palace, The Babylon," pp. 15–37, and "GA Projects: 10 Projects," pp. 38–57, cover.

Florida South Chapter/American Institute of Architects, August 1983, "Buildings Around Town," by Lawrence E. Arrington, AIA, p. 2.

House Beautiful's Home Remodeling, Summer 1983, "Expanded to Open a Cramped Kitchen," pp. 124–25.

Connaissance des Arts (France), September 1983, "Arquitectonica: Une agression totale de le forme," by Philip Johnson, pp. 85–87.

Architecture California, September/October 1983, "G Street Mole Competition," pp. 24–27.

Houston Chronicle, October 9, 1983, "Splashy New Projects Raise Eyebrows," by Mike Sheridan, Section 4, p. 1.

Blueprint: Publication of National Building Museum, "Houston Stunned and Stunning," by Mike Sheridan, Section 4, p. 1.

Texas Architect, November/December 1983, "TSA Design Awards—Twelve Buildings that Represent the Best of Recent Texas Architecture," pp. 58–59.

Miami Herald—Neighbors Magazine, December 4, 1983, "NMB Office Complex May Be Just a Start," by Seth Lebove, p. 2, cover.

Miami Herald, December 6, 1983, "Four Architects Win Awards," by Beth Dunlop.

Miami Herald, December 25, 1983, "Building Up, Tearing Down South Florida's 1983," by Beth Dunlop, p. 7L.

Miami News, December 26, 1983, "Commentary: Miami's Skyline," by Paul Goldberger, p. 9A.

CITE—The Architecture and Design Review of Houston, Winter 1984, "Citelines: Arquitectonica Texas," p. 3.

1984

Artograph/Baruch College, 1984, #4, "Allegro Quality of the Arquitectonica Group," pp. 16–17.

Sun/Coast Architect/Builder, January 1984, "New Wave Architecture."

Texas Architect, January/February 1984, "Dallas to Host Condes' 84" and "The Mesa, Houston, by Arquitectonica," p. 98.

Aboard Viasa, January-April 1984, "Art—The Modern Style," pp. 40–45.

Miami Herald, January 8, 1984, "South Florida's Buildings Will Shine on Tour Sponsored by Architects," p. 30H.

New York Times, January 22, 1984, "Real Estate—Crowning Touch—Sterling Plaza, 255 East 49th Street," Section 8.

Progressive Architecture, February 1984, "In Progress: Banco de Credito, Horizon Hill, and Capital Park West."

Maclean's—Canada's Weekly News Magazine, February 27, 1984, "Architecture: Miami's Brazen New Look," by John Dorschner, p. 62.

Brutus, March 15, 1984, "Research of Asphalt," pp. 121–23.

Miami Herald, March 25, 1984, "A New Spirit for Arquitectonica," by Beth Dunlop, p. 52.

CASA Brutus: Architectural Stylebook Special (Japan), Spring 1984, "Dream Houses," pp. 290–93.

Metropolis—The Architecture and Design Magazine of New York, April 1984, "Knights of Tropical Splendor: A youthful success in an old man's profession—the Miami-based firm of Arquitectonica is bringing its brash, unorthodox design to New York City," by Nori Miller, pp. 15–19, 30, cover.

Inflight, April-May 1984, "Trio of Architects Win Acclaim by Defying the Traditional," by Barbara Johnson, pp. 14–15.

Dallas Morning News, April 15, 1984, "Out of this World in the Grand Prairie: Modern Designers Bring Innovation to Mid-cities Shopping Center," by Steve Brown, Section H, pp. 1–3.

Orlando Sentinel, April 22, 1984, "Miami—A Starlet on the Brink," by Jane Morse, pp. H1-H2.

Dallas/Fort Worth Business, April 30, 1984, "Real Estate Activities (Planets—A Bedrock Development)," p. 22.

Architecture—The Journal of the American Institute of Architects, May 1984, "Seventh Annual Review of New American Architecture," "AIA Components/Florida South Chapter/Atlantis on Brickell," p. 149.

Metropolitan Home, May 1984, "Stylesetters/The Architects—Arquitectonica: Miami Modern," by Robert Cooke Goolrick, p. 79.

NEXT Magazine, May 1984, "Arquitectonica: A Look at New Works by Miami's Gift to Modern American Architecture," by John O'Conner, pp. 5–7.

Inland Architect—The Midwestern Magazine of the Building Arts, May/June 1984, "Modernism: Is It Still Alive?" pp. 17–19.

L'Architecture d'Aujourd'hui (France), June 1984, "La Forme Libre—Centre de Mode, Soho, New York, Arquitectonica," pp. 32–33.

Marquee—South Florida's Magazine, June 1984, "Fame Fortune and Arquitectonica," by Bill Hutchinson, pp. 31–35.

Miami Herald, June 3, 1984, "Island Designs on Tour," Home and Design Section, p. 26H.

Miami Record and Daily Review, July 5, 1984, "New Capital Bank Office Designed by Arquitectonica," p. 1B.

Houston Downtown, July 16, 1984, "Townhouse Trends," by Carmen Keltner, pp. 3–4, 6–8, cover.

Wall Street Journal, July 17, 1984, "Architecture/Arquitectonica: Miami's Architects of Upward Mobility," by Ellen Posner, p. 29.

Miami Today, July 19, 1984, "Brickell Today," p. 1.

Rocky Mountain News, "Town Homes Herald New Wave Architecture—Architect Calls Work 'Romantic,'" July 21, 1984, pp. 6H, 8H.

Time, July 23, 1984, "Design/Jazzing Up the Functional—A Brash Young Miami Firm Offers more than Modernity," by Wolf von Eckerdt, pp. 91–92.

MEMO—Newsletter of the American Institute of Architects, July 26, 1984, "Octagon Fall Lectures to Highlight Design Trends."

Architectural Record, August 1984, "Building Types Study: Multifamily Housing: Haddon Townhouses, Houston, Texas, Arquitectonica, Architects," by Margaret Gaskie, pp. 85–91.

Tampa Tribune, August 5, 1984, "Arquitectonica: Loudly Reshaping America," by Greg Tozian, pp. 1H, 3H, 4H.

New York Magazine, August 6, 1984, "Getting Roofed [Sterling Plaza]", by Amy Virshup, p. 20.

Miami Herald, August 12, 1984, "Spirit and Splendor of South Florida's Architecture," by Beth Dunlop, pp. 1L–4L.

Architectural Record, "Record Interiors," Mid-September 1984, "New Products: Guess who's coming to dinner? Laurinda Spear—Miami Beach," pp. 172–73.

Vogue, October 1984, "Cities/Miami—Arquitectonica . . . becoming the talk of the country's architectural community," by Kathleen Madden, pp. 410–31.

Vogue, October 1984, "Living/Gazette—Big-name Architects Create Exciting Table Accessories," by Barbara Plumb, p. 510.

Texas Architect, September-October 1984, "Taggart Townhouses," by Jim Steely, photography by Richard Payne, pp. 62–65.

L'Architecture d'Aujourd'hui, October 1984, "Arquitectonica: Projets Récents, une Architecture Régionale," pp. 66–81.

Texas Homes, November 1984, "Architecture: Breaking New Ground, the Changing Face of Texas Architecture—Taggart Townhouses, Houston," by Lisa Broadwater, pp. 114–19.

Alas Inflight Group (Antillean Airlines, Faucett Peruvian Airlines, COPA), "Architecture: Designs that Sizzle" and "Arquitectura: Fantasia en el Diseno," by Elizabeth MacLean, pp. 6–14.

Space Design (Japan), November 1984, "Arquitectonica in Miami," pp. 65–76.

Esquire/The Esquire 1984 Registry, December 1984, "The Best of the New Generation: Men and Women Under Forty Who Are Changing America" and "Designs on Miami: Armed with colored pencils and architectural chutzpah, Arquitectonica's partners are remolding the city of the future," by Patricia Leigh Brown, pp. 192–98.

Texas Architect, December 1984, "On Juries and Jurying: Standing in Judgment of Architecture," by Frank Welch, FAIA, pp. 38–39.

Downtown: Renaissance Miami's Arts & Lifestyle Magazine, December 1984, "Changing the Face of Miami's Skyline," by Beth Katz, pp. 20–26.

Miami News, December 5, 1984, "New Design Elements," by Carol Comer, Lifestyle Section B, pp. 1–2.

Miami Herald, December 9, 1984, "Making a Show of Architecture," by Beth Dunlop, pp. 1L, 12L.

Miami Sun Times, December 13, 1984, Cultural Scene, "Arquitectonica," by Barbara Baer Capitman, p. 11.

Miami News, December 14, 1984, Miami Art Scene, "A Bracing Architectural Tonic from Miami's 'Skylinebusters,'" by Dr. Paula Harper, p. 5C.

Time, December 17, 1984, "Their Plates are Smashing," by J.D. Reed, reported by William Tynan.

Trade Wind, vol. 6, no. 4, "Designs that Sizzle," by Elizabeth MacLean, pp. 6–8.

1985

Centers: A Journal for Architecture in America, Center for the Study of American Architecture, School of Architecture, University of Texas at Austin, vol. 1, 1985, "A Proposed Retail District: Arquitectonica" and "The Land, The City and the Human Spirit: Building the Emerging American Landscape," by Larry Paul Fuller, pp. 64–69, 75, 118–21.

Arts and Architecture, vol. 3, no. 3, "Houston Townhouses," by Stephen Fox, pp. 60–65.

Artograph/Baruch College, no. 4, "Massimo Vignelli," pp. 16–17.

International Herald Tribune-Weekend, January 4, 1985, "The Celebrity Architect Arrives," by Paul Goldberger.

Montrose Voice, January 11, 1985, "Arquitectonica—The City as Art," by Jeff Bray, Montrose Art, p. 14.

La Razon (Buenos Aires, Argentina), January 15, 1985, "Tresnovenes transforman el perfil urbano de Miami," p. 30.

Texas Monthly, January 1985, "Strident Whimsey," by Lisa Germany, pp. 124–29.

New Woman, February 1985, "Who's News—Laurinda Spear: Architect par Excellence," by Barbaralee Diamonstein, p. 32.

Texas Homes, vol. 9, no. 2, "Editor's Notebook—Arquitectonica Hits the Dallas Homefront," p. 16.

Houston Post, February 3, 1985, "The Zephyr Arrives with Fresh Paint," p. 32.

Newsweek, February 4, 1985, "Architecture—Designing with Sly Wit," by Douglas Davis, pp. 76–77.

Architektur und Technik (West Germany), February 1985, cover.

Time, February 4, 1985, "Design—The Battle of Starship Chicago," by Richard Lacayo, reported by Christopher Ogden/Chicago, p. 84.

Dallas Times Herald, February 7, 1985, "Unique Building Designed for Dallas," by Ruth Eyre, Business, pp. B1 and B3.

House Beautiful, February 1985, "HB Lookout—Madonna Lacquered Wood Table, Designed by Laurinda Spear," p. 23.

Miami Herald, February 26, 1985, "House goes Hollywood," by Christopher Wellisz, Local News, p. 1D.

Techniques et Architecture (France), no. 358, "Deux Réalisations Récentes d'Arquitectonica," pp. 17–19.

Miami Herald, March 1, 1985, "Watson Boating Center Proposed," by Neil Brown, pp. 1–2D.

Miami News, March 1, 1985, "Foe Gives Cautious OK to Watson Island Plan," by Bill Gjerbe.

Miami Herald, March 10, 1985, "Arquitectonica Designs Patio Homes," Home and Design, p. 33H.

Miami Herald, March 10, 1985, "Watson Island Proposal—Too Much of a Good Thing," by Beth Dunlop, p. 2L.

Aero Peru, vol. 1, no. 1, "Architecture—Designs that Sizzle," by Elizabeth MacClain, pp. 6–8, and "Arquitectura—Fantasia en El Diseño," pp. 9–10.

Houston Chronicle, March 17, 1985, "Moving Experiences for Houston Galleries," by Patricia C. Johnson, Art, p. 17.

New York, March 25, 1985, "The High Style of Miami Vice," by Wendy Goodman, photographed by Douglas Keeve, pp. 54–65.

Miami News, March 26, 1985, "Ins & Outs," by Mort Lucoff, p. 15A.

Modernismi Murtuu (Finland), by Mieja Sassi, pp. 196–99.

Miami Herald, Home and Design, March 10, 1985, "Cocoplovis: The Last Holdout on Brickell," by Jo Werne, pp. 1H, 12H, 13H [The Junior League Showhouse].

Dallas Times Herald, March 24, 1985, "Bradley Bayoud," by Ron Boyd, Unique, pp. 1, 2.

Architectes Architecture (France), April 1985, "Le Discourse des Architectes Toniques [Atlantis, Horizon Hill]," pp. 20–23, cover.

Texas Homes, May 1985, "Architecture—Taggart Townhouses," p. 54.

Architectural Record, June 1985, "Building Types Study 615: Townhouses—Those New Kids in Town," by Charles K. Gandee, pp. 117–33.

Platinum Card Review, American Express, June 1985, "Setting Precedents: New Corporate Architecture," p. 43.

Progressive Architecture, June 1985, "In Progress—Synodinos House, Indian Creek Island, Florida, Vilaseca House, Guayaquil, Ecuador," p. 43.

Engineering News-Record, June 6, 1985, "Design Diversity Brings Obstacles, Opportunities [Bayoud Flatiron]," pp. 22–25, cover.

Southern Homes, Tampa Bay edition, Summer 1985, "Arquitectonica," pp. 52–63.

Houston Post, July 6, 1985, "Houston Galleries on the Move," Section G, p. 1.

Miami Herald, July 7, 1985, "Building or Furniture, Architects Love Designing," Section H, p. 6.

Miami Review, July 8, 1985. "Corporate Report—Arquitectonica Products," p. 6.

Vogue, August 1985, "Time Profiles," p. 295, and "International Timetables," p. 63.

Sky, Delta Air Lines Inflight Magazine, August 1985, "A Symphony in Structure," p. 63.

Signature, August 1985, "Miami Sights," p. 37.

Wall Street Journal, August 5, 1985, "Success of Flashy 'Miami Vice' TV Show May Be Rubbing Off on Troubled Miami," Section 2, p. 1.

Newsweek, August 12, 1985, "The Wilder Shore of Design," p. 64.

City Magazine International, August 1985, "Arquitectonica," pp. 79–82.

Metropolitan Home, September 1985, "Hot Properties—Miami," p. 16.

Staten Island Advance, August 2, 1985, "Seven Bidding on South Ferry's Future," pp. 1, 9.

Engineering News-Record, August 29, 1985. "Site in Water No Deterrent [South Ferry Plaza]," pp. 13–14.

Miami Herald, September 16, 1985, "Silver Knights for Adults," Spirit of Excellence Awards.

Tropic Magazine, September 22, 1985, "Eight Who Made a Difference."

Village Voice, October 1, 1985, "Ferry Godfathers," by Michael Sorkin, p. 94.

Metropolis, October 1985, Annual Design Review—1985, "Scene & Heard—Assault and Battery [South Ferry Plaza]," p. 10, and "Furnishings, From Wool to Wall," p. 55.

Newsday, October 10, 1985, "At Home—Women in Architecture," by Barbara Flanagan, pp. 10–11.

Art Deco Society Pictorial, October 20, 1985, "Port of Miami Revisited."

Metropolis, November 1985, "Tropical Retail [Arquitectonica Products]," p. 14, and "Critics on Criticism, What the Architects Say," pp. 29–30.

Homes, November 14, 1985, "Today's Special Profile—Laurinda Spear Designs Homes for Arquitectonica."

Miami Today, November 21, 1985, "Arquitectonica Selected to Design Port Complex," by Pat Broderick.

Progressive Architecture, December 1985, "P/A News Report—South Ferry Plaza: Jury Still Out," p. 21.

GA Document (Japan), December 1985, "Mesa East," pp. 74–75.

Chicago Tribune, December 1, 1985, "Architecture—Grande Dame of Art Deco Decries the Yuppie Invasion of Miami Beach," by Paul Gapp, Section 13, p. 16.

Miami Today, December 12, 1985, "Brickell to Get Riverfront Built Apartments," by Pat Broderick.

Miami Herald, December 20, 1985, "New Office Complex to be Built at Port [Dodge Island, Miami]," by Dory Owens, p. 2C.

1986

Metropolitan Home, January 1986, "More on Moore, Bernardo Fort-Brescia: Moore's Influence on American Architecture Today," p. 23.

Progressive Architecture, January 1986, "P/A Awards Update: Winners Rise," pp. 140–43.

Miami Herald, January 12, 1986, "New Models—Arquitectonica Model Opens [Mandalay at Boca Pointe]," Section H, p. 22.

South Florida Home and Garden, February 1986, "In House—Made in China [Miami Beach plate by Laurinda Spear]," by Rosemary Barrett, p. 18.

Process Architecture no. 65 (Japan), February 1986, "Romantic Modernism: Arquitectonica," pp. 1–135.

U.S. News & World Report, February 24, 1986, "The Struggle to Regain Paradise Lost," by Stewart Powell, pp. 21–22.

Daily Pennsylvanian, March 1986, "Art-chitecture—'Avantegarde' Work Displayed at Institute," by Leslie Kerr, pp. 21–22.

Maritime Reporter & Engineering News, March 1986, "$31 Million Development Project Begins at Port of Miami," p. 9.

Philadelphia Inquirer, March 18, 1986, "Since These Young Miami Architects Can Do It, They Do," by Thomas Hine, Entertainment/Art, pp. 1-J, 14-J.

Cruise Industry News, March 19, 1986, "Expansion Projects at Port of Miami to Support Burgeoning Cruise Industry," pp. 1, 3.

Marine Digest, March 22, 1986, "Cruise Industry Stimulates Port of Miami Expansion."

Real Estate Weekly, March 24, 1986, "$31 Million Port of Miami Project Reflects Public-Private Initiatives," p. 18.

New York Newsday, March 27, 1986, "City Living—Young Minds Break the Mold," pp. 5, 8.

Pennsylvania Gazette, April 1986, "Miami Virtue, Arquitectonica," pp. 30–31.

Process: Architecture (Japan), April 1986, "The Imperial," pp. 164–65.

Architectural Record, April 1986, "Arquitectonica for Sale," pp. 104–107.

Architectural Record, mid-April 1986, "Record Houses—In a Secret Garden," by Douglas Brenner, pp. 80–89.

Atlanta Neighbor, April 9, 1986, "Innovative Shopping Entertainment Complex Planned," by Arlie Porter, Business, p. 6C.

Miami Today, April 10, 1986, "Today's Profile—Jorge Arguelles, We Concentrate on Making the Client Feel at Home," p. 4.

FP Magazine, May 1986, "Design/USA: Report on Design Trends in the U.S.," pp. 53–55.

Miami Herald, May 18, 1986, "America's Cities Lack Individuality in Design," by Christopher Boyd, Home and Design, p. 1H–16H.

Houston City Magazine, June 1986, "The Houston Look," pp. HL10–16.

South Florida Home & Gardens, June 1986, "Turn the Tables," by Rosemary Barrett, p. 70.

Midtown Business Journal, June 1986, "RIO: Midtown's New Entertainment and Shopping Center," p. 2, cover.

On the Avenue, June 1986, "Miami Slice," by Allen Veter.

Architecture and Urbanism, July 1986, "South Ferry Plaza Competition," pp. 12–14.

Miami Review, August 2, 1986, "Close But No Cigar," by Jan Sandusky, pp. 1, 3.

South Florida Business Journal, October 6, 1986, "Tenant List Grows as Bayside Marketplace Takes Place," p. 20.

Emerging Voices, September 1986, "Laurinda Spear/Arquitectonica," pp. 30–31.

Interiors Magazine, September 1986, "40 Under 40," p. 158.

Vogue Décoration (France), September 1986, "Ordre à Lima," by Christine Colin, pp. 146–51.

Kleur en Architectuur (The Netherlands), September 28-October 9, 1986, exhibition catalog in Museum Boymans-von Beuningen, Rotterdam, The Netherlands, pp. 172–73.

Miami Herald, October 24, 1986, "Coral Way Shopping Mall OK'd," by Justin Gillis and Reinald Ramos, p. 2C.

L'Architecttura (Italy), November 1986, "Quattro Case Dello Studio Arquitectonica," by Giancarlo Priori, pp. 38–41.

Sidewalk Superintendent, November 1986, "Mid-Atlantic Region to Build Center for Innovative Technology," p. 6.

Miami Review, November 7, 1986, "Architecture on the Fantastic," by Phillip Stelly, p. 7.

1987

Architecture Contemporaine (Switzerland), no. 8 (1987), "Seamark at the Port," pp. 114–16.

Miami Today, January 15, 1987, "Developers Bring New Life to Beach," by Mary E. Karrer, p. 10.

Haüser (Germany), January 1987, "An Architectural Gem Behind High Walls in Lima," by Horst Rash, pp. 12–19.

New Yorker, May 18, 1987, "A Reporter at Large: The Second Havana," by David Rieff, pp. 65–83.

Interiors, June 1986, "Law Unto Itself: Colson Hicks and Edison Office by Arquitectonica," by Paula Rice Jackson, pp. 180–85.

Miami Herald, June 14, 1987, "Modernism vs. Post-Modernism," by Beth Dunlop, Fine Arts Section.

Miami Herald (Broward County edition), June 14, 1987, "Mall's Specifics Kept Secret," by David Medzerian, Section B, p. 1.

Fortune, June 22, 1987, "Architects for the 1990s," by Brian Dumain, pp. 152–53.

Miami Herald, June 20, 1987, "Brickell, A Mirror of Miami," by Beth Dunlop, pp. 1K, 6K.

Miami Review, July 30, 1987, "Arquitectonica's Miracle on Coral Way," by Alex Finklestein, p. 4.

Miami Today, July 30, 1987, "Arquitectonica—Spanish for Architecture," p. 9.

Architectural Digest, Architecture Supplement, September 1987, "Miami's Arquitectonica: Merging Two Penthouses in Firm's Palace Highrise," by Steven M. Aronson, pp. 46–52.

Tropical Splendor, An Architectural History of Florida, by Hap Hatton (New York: Alfred A. Knopf, 1987), pp. 120–23.

Miami Herald, December 13, 1987, "Bold Hall of Fame Design Sure to Make a Splash," by Beth Dunlop, p. 8K.

Miami Herald Broward News, December 8, 1987, "Center Plunges into $7.2 Million Face Lift," by Darrek Eiland, p. 1B.

Fort Lauderdale News, December 8, 1987, "Plans Unveiled to Rebuild Swimming Hall of Fame," by Nancy I. Roman, p. 1B.

Miami News, December 8, 1987, "Lauderdale Plans Tourist Center," by Ivonne Rovira, p. 8.

L'Architecture d'Aujourd'hui (France), October 1987, "Sous la Lumier Andine," pp. 88–89.

1988

Miami: City of The Future, by T. D. Allman, (New York: The Atlantic Monthly Press), pp. 34–41.

GA Houses, January 1988, Special Issue #2, "Walner House."

Hi-Riser, January 7, 1988, "Swimming Hall of Fame to be Revamped," pp. 1–3.

ENR, January 14, 1988, "Oddly Shaped Frames Poured Fast [CIT]," p. 17.

Pompano Ledger, January 21, 1988, "Swimming Hall of Fame Unveils New Wave for the Future," p. 8A.

Architectural Record, January 1988, "Miami's Northern Lights," p. 33.

South Florida Business Journal, January 1988, "Biggest Land Deals [Sawgrass Mills]," by Sarene Collins, p. 36.

Miami Today, February 4, 1988, "Babylon Is OK For Occupancy," by Cindy Goodwin, p. 2.

Miami Herald, February 14, 1988, "New Courthouse to Open Tuesday," by Kathy McCarthy, p. 4.

Miami Herald, Neighbors, February 18, 1988, "You Judge the Results," p. 16.

Miami Herald, February 21, 1988, "Verdict on Courthouse: Delightful," by Beth Dunlop, p. 4K.

New York Times, February 21, 1988, "In The Spirit Of Carnival [Rio]," by Michael Pousner.

Miami Review, February 25, 1988, "Justices Not Blind to Arquitectonica's Talent," by John Sugg, p. 2.

Miami Today, February 25, 1988, "Miracle Center Forges Ahead," by Cindy Goodwin, p. 7.

Miami Today, February 25, 1988, "Arquitectonica Drafting Plans for Florida's Biggest Mall," by Cindy Goodwin, p. 10.

Travelhost, February 28, 1988, "International Swimming Hall of Fame."

New River Times Magazine, February 1988, "Hall of Fame to Expand," p. 17.

Waterfront News, February 1988, "Swimming Hall of Fame Unveils New Wave for the Future," by Colleen Mahouney, p. 22.

Profit, February/March 1988, "A New Wave on the Beach," pp. 52–54.

Sunshine, The Magazine of South Florida, March 13, 1988, "Vice Is Nice," by Roberta Klein, pp. 19–21.

Miami Today, March 31, 1988, "Players in Place for a New Brickell Called Coral Way," by Cindy Goodman.

Miami Today, March 31, 1988, "Imperial's Sales Run Ahead of Target," by Cindy Goodwin, p. 9.

Stern, March 30, 1988, "Journal Bauen, Wohnen und Garten," pp. 171–80.

Domus, March 1988, "Casa los Andes [Mulder House]," by Vittorio Magnago Lampugnani, pp. 25–32.

Construction, April 11, 1988, "Splayed Column Design, Tight Schedule Challenge Contractor on CIT Complex," pp. 30–32.

Fulton County Daily Report, April 18, 1988, "Rio," by Tom Chaffin, p. 1.

Archis, April 1988, "Form Follows Fancy," pp. 16–25.

Florida Trend, April 1988, "Biscayne Creditbank Tower," p. 67.

Häuser, April 1988, "Architekten: Im Duett Gegen den Strom," p. 8.

House & Garden, April 1988, "Then-Now," p. 135.

Cultural Quarterly, vol 1., no. 2 (Spring Issue, 1988), "Diving Into Design."

Florida Architect, March/April 1988, "New Commissions [NDJC]," p. 7.

Häuser, April 1988, "Architekten: Im Duett Gegen Den Strom," p. 8.

Miami Herald, May 1, 1988, "Concrete Dreams," by Beth Dunlop, p. 1K.

South Florida Business Journal, May 2, 1988, "Top 25 Construction Projects in the South Florida Region," p. 18.

Wall Street Journal, May 13, 1988, "Form and Function (and an Unlikely Place For Fancy Architecture)," by Stephen MacDonald, p. 21.

New York Times, May 26, 1988, "Where Corridors of Justice are Curved," by Patricia Leigh Brown, p. 14C.

Architectural Record, May 1988, "Miami Virtue," by Paul Sachner, pp. 123–29.

Eastern Review, May 1988, "Miami In May," by Molly Staub, p. 30.

Horizon, May 1988, "No Exceptions," by Marcia J. Wade, pp. 33–40.

Pulse, May 1988, "Arquitectonica in Broward County, Bernardo Fort-Brescia Talks about His Work [ISHOF]," p. 3.

Florida Architect, May/June 1988, "A Sculpted House Hides the Street," pp. 20–21.

National Masters Magazine, May/June 1988, "The New Swimming Hall of Fame," p. 11.

Miami Today, June 2, 1988, "Miracle Center Lures Big Names into 17-Story Coral Way Complex," by Cindy Krischer Goodman.

Miami Today, June 30, 1988, "The Best of Miami—Choosing the Best of Our Condos is Easy . . . Just a Matter of Taste [Atlantis & Palace]," pp. 22–23.

Architectural Record, June 1988, "Atlanta: Power Shopping for the New Urban Gentry [Rio]," p. 65.

Metropolitan Home, June 1988, "Bay Dreams," by Arlene Hirst, p. 20.

Eastern Review, July 1988, "A Neighborly Sort of Place," by Caskie Stinnett, p. 23–46.

South Florida Business Journal, July 4, 1988, "Top 25 Most Expensive Condominiums in South Florida," p. 48.

Time, July 11, 1988, "Earth and Fire, Latin Flair Adds Color and Spice to American Styles," by Nancy R. Gibbs, pp. 68–71.

Miami Today, July 21, 1988, "The People Who Make Things Happen on Brickell Avenue," by M. J. Taylor, p. 13.

Miami Today, July 28, 1988, "West Coconut Grove Area Targeted for Major Revamp [Grove Point]," Linda Rodriguez Bernfeld, p. 3.

Metropolis, July/August 1988, "The Birds & The Boys," p. 28.

SD, August 1988, Center for Innovative Technology, International Swimming Hall of Fame.

Baltimore Sun, August 14, 1988, "Reflecting Innovation and Technology," by Edward Gunts, pp. 1N, 3N.

New Times, August 16, 1988, "Aquatexture," pp. 16–17.

San Francisco Examiner, August 21, 1988, "Miami Nice," by Patricia Beach Smith, pp. F7–8.

Ambiente, August 26, 1988, "Ein Star in Rosa [Spear House]," by Martin Filler, pp. 110–16.

Art in America, September 1988, "Power Skyline," by Paula Harper, pp. 55–65.

Miami Herald, September 1988, "Coral Way Super Mall Almost Done," by Jeffrey Kleinman, Neighbors, p. 3.

South Florida Business Journal, September 5, 1988, "Top 250 Office Spaces in South Florida Area," p. 18.

New York Times, September 15, 1988, "How Do New Gardens Grow? In Green Sand and Fantasy," by Daralice D. Boles. p. C1.

Architectural Record, Mid-September 1988, "New Products," pp. 128–29.

South Florida Business Journal, October 3, 1988, "Top 25 Architectural Firms in the South Florida Area," p. 22.

GA Houses #23, "Mandell, Summit," pp. 198–203.

Domus, November 1988, "Arquitectonica, Sede del Banco de Credito, Lima," pp. 31–35.

Connoisseur, November 1988, "Glamour, Inc. Arquitectonica with the Latino Flash," Walter McQuade.

House & Garden, November 1988, "Miami on Lake Michigan," by Charles Gandee, pp. 170–77.

Town & Country, November 1988, "Miami's Cultural Boom—Making over Miami."

Vanidades, vol. 28, no. 22, "Arquitectura," p. 10.

Miami Today, November 10, 1988, "Miracle Center's Opening Put Off Until February, 90 Percent Leased," by Cindy Goodman, p. 26.

Designweek, November 11, 1988, "Florida Hall of Fame at a Stroke."

Atlanta Constitution, November 13, 1988, "Eye Catcher—Splashy Design Makes Waves for Rio Retail Center," by Catherine Fox, pp. 1K, 2K.

Miami Herald, November 14, 1988, "Miami-style Mall Jolts Atlantans," by Fred Grimm, pp. 1A, 4A.

Miami Herald, November 23, 1988, "Miami Shows its Local Color," by Peggy Landers, pp. 1D–2D.

News-Sun, November 29, 1988, "Big Jim D.C. Bound, One Observer Says [Gurnee Mills]," Section 1, p. 3.

Guarantor, November/December 1988, "Sawgrass Mills Brings Alternative Mall to Florida," pp. 4–6.

Historic Preservation, November/December 1988, "New Clout for Historic Districts," by Howard Mansfield, p. 23.

1989

Business Week, January 9, 1989, "The Best of Architecture—Mall of Fame," p. 129.

Museum & Arts, January/February 1989, "Arquitectonica's Designs on D.C.," p. 13.

Architectural Record, February 1989, "Bankers' Trust," by Karen Stein, pp. 90–100, cover.

Florida Trend, February 1989, "The Achievers—Where Are They Now?" p. 35.

Chicago Tribune, February 18, 1989, "Builder's Art," pp. 1C–2C.

Miami Today, February 23, 1989, "Round-the-Clock Work Paves Way for Miracle Center Debut," by Cindy Goodman, p. 11.

Miami Herald, February 26, 1989, "South Florida's Architects Merit World Renown," by Beth Dunlop, p. 5K.

Häuser, March 1989, "Hommage à Richard Ludwig van der Corbusier [Banco de Credito]" pp. 30–37.

Houston Metropolitan, March 1989, "Mystery Building," pp. 9–10.

Kateigaho, March 1989, "Pink House on Biscayne Bay," pp. 180–88.

Casa Vogue, vol. 13, no. 1, "Um Mergulho No Moderno," by Jay Weinfeld, p. 20.

W Magazine, March 6–13, 1989, "The Wit and Wisdom of Arquitectonica," by Pat Kivestu.

Postmortem, March 21, 1989, "Bernardo Fort-Brescia and Laurinda Spear," p. 5.

Miami Today, March 23, 1989, "More Miracle Centers on Schoenberg's Wish List," p. 4.

Dallas Morning News, March 25, 1989, "Exotic Elevator Crows and Glows," by Lydia Martin, pp. 1C, 3C.

Eigen Huis & Interieur, April 1989, "Poetisch Bouwen In Miami," pp. 98–103.

Metropolitan Home, April 1989, "Secrets of the City," pp. 60–63.

Weekend Australian, April 1, 1989, "Como May Go Avant Garde," by Grant Muller.

Washington Post, April 8, 1989, "The Topsy-Turvy Tower of Power," by Benjamin Forgey, pp. C1, C4.

Chicago Tribune, April 9, 1989, "Building Tension," by Paul Gapp, Section 13, p. 4.

Las Vegas Review, April 9, 1989, "Elevator Passengers are Treated to a Unique Symphony, Light Show," p. 11A.

Chicago Tribune, April 10, 1989, "Sinking Expectations."

Miami Herald, April 13, 1989, "New Snapper Creek Plazas to Serve Hungry Drivers," by Jon O'Neil, pp. K10–11.

Interiors, May 1989, "Peru Strikes Gold," by Beverly Russell, pp. 89–93.

Miami Herald, May 21, 1989, "In Vice We Found Our Virtues," by Beth Dunlop, p. 4K.

Atlanta Constitution, May 21, 1989, "Video Vexation," by Catherine Fox, pp. L1, L6.

Building Design, May 26 1989, "Miami Modernist," p. 2.

El Ingeniero Civil, May/June 1989, "Banco de Credito del Peru, Nueva Sede La Molina," pp. 30–32, cover.

SF Magazine, premiere issue, 1989, "A Winery Before its Time," p. 16.

Identity, Spring 1989, "Rio, A Different Angle," pp. 50–53.

Design South, vol. 12, no. 4 (1989), "Celebrating 15 Years of Good Design," p. 65.

Progressive Architecture, June 1989, "Presenting Ideas," pp. 84–86.

Connaissance des Arts, June 1989, "Le Temple du Soleil."

Atlanta Constitution, June 9, 1989, "Old and New Honored with Urban Design Commission Awards [Rio]," by Catherine Fox, pp. B1, B4.

Nikkei Architecture, June 26, 1989, "Banco de Credito," pp. 216–27.

Miami Magazine, Summer 1989, "Tropical Architecture," by Louis Mejia, pp. 8–9.

1/2 de Construccion, May/June 1989, "Banco de Credito," pp. 13–15, cover.

Progressive Architecture, June 1989, "Rio Shopping Center/International Swimming Hall of Fame," pp. 64–65.

Abitare, July/August 1989, "South Dade Miracle," pp. 156–57, and "North Dade—Corte de Giustizia," pp. 162–63.

Casa Vogue, Luglio/Agosto 1989, "Ricominciando da Zeta [Walner House]," by Paolo Rinaldi, pp. 68–73.

Miami Today, May 25, 1989, "Now playing at your theatre: Invasion of the Multi-plexes."

Designer's West, August 1989, "Innovative Floorscapes," pp. 110–11.

Progressive Architecture, August 1989, "Rio/Center for Innovative Technology."

Miami Herald, August 27, 1989, "New Rest Stops for the Weary Rise Above the Dreary," by Beth Dunlop, pp. 1K–6K.

Nikkei Architecture, September 1989, pp. 238–43.

Miami Herald, September 5, 1989, "Turnpike Plazas Reopen in Style," by Richard Hart.

Florida Architect, September/October 1989, "1989 FA/AIA Awards for Excellence in Architecture," pp. 9, 22–54, cover.

Newsweek, October 1989, "The Great Outdoors," by Maggie Malone, pp. 44–45.

Miami Herald, October 22, 1989, "Miami Lights," by Beth Dunlop, Section H.

Architecture Intérieure Créé, M 1307–231, "Un Palais . . . Post Aztech [Banco de Credito]," pp. 132–40.

Smithsonian, November 1989, "Elevating Thoughts from Elisha Otis and Fellow Uplifters," by Donald Dale Jackson, pp. 211–33.

AAA World, November/December 1989, "Miami's Architectural Delights," by Betsy Rubin, pp. 2b–2e.

1990

Architektur des 20. Jahrhunderts, 1990, "Arquitectonica—The Atlantis," pp. 344–45.

Architectural Record, January 1990, "Bank Job," by Karen Stein, p. 21.

Basa, January 1990, "Edificio de Juzgados del Condado de Dade," pp. 38–43.

Hauser, January 1990, "Controlled Chaos," pp. 100–104.

Hauser, March 1990, "Geldadel: Architecturperle fur Luxemburg," p. 10.

Quaderns d'Arquitectura i Urbanisme 185, April-May-June 1990, "Arquitectonica: Interview, Rio Shopping Center, North Dade Justice Center, Center for Innovative Technology, Banco de Credito," pp. 40–71.

Hauser, June 1990, "Dies ist ein Ganz Normales Haus.," pp. 44–50.

Arquitectura Viva, September-October 1990, "Escenografia en el paramo, Arquitectonica: de Miami a Lima," pp. 24–28.

New York Times, October 25, 1990, "Having a Wonderful Time in Miami," Home, p. C1.

Baumeister, October 1990, "Neues aus L.A.," pp. 36–41.

Miami Herald, November 11, 1990, "Family Lifestyle," p. 1J.

Orlando Sentinel, November 17, 1990, "Miami's Tropical Trimmings: Architect's Home Delivers Florida Image," Homes, pp. G1, G13.

Miami Herald, December 16, 1990, "With Orange Peels and Lasers, Tree Designers Make Merry," p. 9J.

Time, December 17, 1990, "The Price is Always Right," pp. 66–68.

Architectural Digest, December 1990, "Arquitectonica at Home," pp. 42–54.

Miami Review, December 14, 1990, "Rockin' Round the Christmas Trees," p. 16.

Metamorfosi, Interni-Esterni Metropolitani, 1990, "Metropolitan Culture—Banco de Credito," pp. 55–57.

1991

Immeubles de Bureaux, Editions du Moniteur, 1991, "Arquitectonica. Banque de Crédit du Perou, Lima," pp. 46–49.

Inland Architect, January 1991, "Architecture by Women: Arquitectonica, Coral Gables," pp. 30, 31.

Metropolitan Home, January 1991, "Miami Mischief," pp. 51–57.

Washington Post, January 12, 1991, "Cityscape: Along the Road to Rio," Style, pp. D1, D7.

Techniques & Architecture, March 1991, Banque de Luxembourg, pp. 118, 119, 124, 125.

Miami Herald, April 28, 1991, "Tile—International Exposition Borders on the Fantastic with Fantasy Video Rooms, Video and More," Home & Design, pp. 1G, 4G.

Miami Herald, May 12, 1991, "A Style of Our Own," Arts, pp. 1I, 8I.

Acknowledgments

Bernardo Fort-Brescia and Laurinda Spear wish to acknowledge the collaboration of the following individuals:

Andres Duany
Principal, 1977–79

Elizabeth Plater-Zyberk
Principal, 1977–79

Hervin A.R. Romney
Principal, 1977–84

Sergio Bakas
Thomas Bittner
M. Jenifer Briley
Enrique Chuy
Bill Holt, Jr.
Bradford Korder
Richard Perlmutter
Dana Terp
Robert S. Tolmach, Jr.
Carlos Prio Touzet
Martin Wander
Carl H. Young III

Mario Alvarez
Peter Alvarez
Paula Anderson
Natalye Appel
Samira Azgua
Paul Barke
Yara Bashoor
Beatrice H. Bastidas
Olivier Baudry
Stuart W. Baur
Heidi Behr
Peter Blackburn
Roger Bolling
José Bon
Guillermo Brunzini
Santiago Bustamante
Sergio Canton
Amauri Chacon
Gustavo Chuy
Alexander Chun
Donna M. Clous
Marc Compton
Ronald Cox
Juan Carlos David
Michael Dax
Nurys M. Decreouy
Deborah Desilets
George M. Despues
David Digiacomo
Eduardo J. Dorta
Tony Engelberg
Olga Espinosa
Theodore M. Evangelakis
Sandra Fandre
Maurice Farinas
Diana Farmer
Gigi Fernandez
Ricardo Fernandez
William B. Fitzpatrick
Frederick Fleshman
Raymond John Fowler
Robin Hamilton Fyfe
Robert Gallagher
George L. Garcia
Caridad Hidalgo-Gato
John R. Glagola
Marjorie Goldman
Annette Gonzalez
Edgar Gonzalez
Willis A. Gortner II
Andy Gruber
Juan Carlos Guerrero
Daphne I. Gurri
Candi Gutierrez
Judith Haase
Michael Halland
Shahrixan Amir Hamzah
Geron Lee Harrison
Erik M. Hemingway
Michael Heron
Lidia E. Heres
George Hernandez

Violeta Hernandez
Ava Dawn Hetzer
Jamison Heyliger
Jane Hobbs
Michel Holland
Brad Hollenbeck
Bill Holt
Ismail B. Imran
Yehuda E. Inbar
Daniel Irizarry
Alfredo Julien
Peter Kiernan
Scott Kirk
David Kocieniewski
Viviane Fort Korder
Irene M. Kulis
Francisco Laurier
Karoline Leuenberger
Michael D. Liss
Rolando Llanes
Eduardo Llano
Eduardo Luaces
Nicholas Lucarelli
Douglas W. Mar
Ana Marin
John Maruszczak
José Matute
Mark Maccagno
Edmond MacLeod Maurice
Kathy McMurphy
Jonathan Meyers
Francisco Miguez, Jr.
Ziyad Mneimneh
Marcelo Moino
Juan A. Montalvan, Jr.
Armando Montero
Arturo Montoya
Antonio Moreno
Cinda M. Morris
Inaki Muguruza
Luisa Murai
George Murillo
Consuelo Noguer
Jésus Novoa
Margarita V. Nuvhe
Anna M. Oppel
Maria Elena Ortega
Schinichi Ozawa
Lisa M. Padilla
Louis Pedraza
Olga Barbara Penalver
Esther Perez
Ileana Perez
Gonzalo Peschiera
Kriss A. Peterson
Grace Pierce
Campion A. Platt
Magda Polec
Raphael Portuondo
Bradley R. Potts
Roberto Roca
David Ramer

Claudio R. Ramos
Janice Rauzin
Suchi Reddy
Joaquin Riera
Brian Robertson
Camilo Rosales
Mercedes Rosales
Jaime R. Rouillon
Joan Ruffe
John Sacco
Derek Sanders
Neal Schefil
Gregory Schenker
Neal A. Schofel
Russell Sherman
Ailsa Simone
Alison L. Spear
Saskia Suite-Hardt
Raphael Sixto
Richard Smart
Alastair Standing
Michael Steffens
Leif Stigson
Ana M. Tejidor
Victoria Teofilo
Robert Thompson
Ruben Travieso
Rafael A. Torrens III
David Trautman
Armando Trujillo
Michael Paul Vascellaro
Maria Gabriela Velutini
Mark Volpendesta
Pierre Walgenwitz
John Watkins
Osvaldo Valdes
Marek Walczak
Julio C. Webel-Valls
James Wells
Gerald West
Allen Wilson
Allen G. Wipon
Dennis Witnauer
Carl Young
Dan Zabowski

We also want to acknowledge the collaboration of these joint venture and associated architects:
Ward/Hall Associates, Fairfax, Virginia, on the Center for Innovative Technology
Milton Pate & Associates, Atlanta, Georgia, on Rio
William Dorsky & Associates, Miami, Florida, on The Palace

Photo Credits

Raymond Bouley	111
Steven Brooke/©Architectural Digest	202–205
Patricia Fisher	92–93, 99, 119, 141–47, 164–67, 176, 178–79
Y. Futagawa/Retoria	28–29, 34–35
Andy Gruber	184–85, 188–89, 192–93
Bill Holt	96–97
Timothy Hursley	23–26, 30–31, 46–49, 56–57, 62–81, 85–89, 101–109, 122–39, 154, 157–61, 170, 172–75
Christopher Janney	120–21
Robert Lautman	4–7, 17
John R. Lawrence	10
Norman McGrath	19–21, 27, 37–45
Richard Payne	55, 83
Rion Rizzo/Creative Sources	112–17
Maggie Silverstein	214
Tim Street-Porter	8, 12–15
Paul Warchol	94–95
Kate Zari	9, 16